BOOK 3

Play Your Scales
and Chords Every Day®
by Helen Marlais

T H E
F·J·H
M U S I C
COMPANY
I N C.
Frank J. Hackinson

Production: Frank J. Hackinson
Production Coordinators: Peggy Gallagher and Philip Groeber
Cover: Terpstra Design, San Francisco
Text Design and Layout: Andi Whitmer
Engraving: Tempo Music Press, Inc.
Printer: Tempo Music Press, Inc.

ISBN-13: 978-1-61928-020-5

ABOUT THE AUTHOR

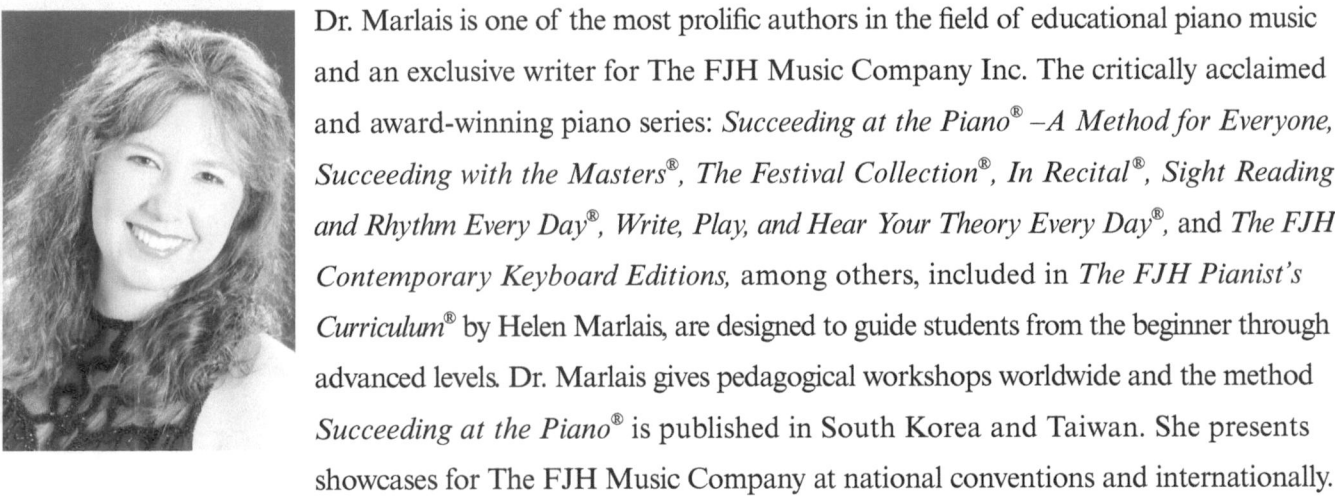

Dr. Marlais is one of the most prolific authors in the field of educational piano music and an exclusive writer for The FJH Music Company Inc. The critically acclaimed and award-winning piano series: *Succeeding at the Piano®* –*A Method for Everyone, Succeeding with the Masters®, The Festival Collection®, In Recital®, Sight Reading and Rhythm Every Day®, Write, Play, and Hear Your Theory Every Day®,* and *The FJH Contemporary Keyboard Editions,* among others, included in *The FJH Pianist's Curriculum®* by Helen Marlais, are designed to guide students from the beginner through advanced levels. Dr. Marlais gives pedagogical workshops worldwide and the method *Succeeding at the Piano®* is published in South Korea and Taiwan. She presents showcases for The FJH Music Company at national conventions and internationally.

Dr. Marlais has performed and presented throughout the U.S. and in Canada, Italy, England, France, Hungary, Turkey, Germany, Lithuania, Estonia, Australia, New Zealand, China, South Korea, Taiwan, Jamaica, and Russia. She has recorded on Gasparo, Centaur and Audite record labels with her husband, concert clarinetist Arthur Campbell. Their recording, *Music for Clarinet and Piano,* was nominated for the 2013 *International Classical Music Awards,* one of the most prestigious distinctions available to classical musicians today. She has also recorded numerous educational piano CD's for Stargrass Records®. She has performed with members of the Chicago, Pittsburgh, Minnesota, Grand Rapids, Des Moines, Cedar Rapids, and Beijing National Symphony Orchestras, and has premiered many new works by contemporary composers from the United States, Canada, and Europe.

Dr. Marlais received her DM in piano performance and pedagogy from Northwestern University, her MFA in piano performance from Carnegie Mellon University, and was awarded the Outstanding Alumna in the Arts from the University of Toledo, where she received her bachelor of music degree in piano performance. As well as being the Director of Keyboard Publications for The FJH Music Company, Dr. Marlais is also an Associate Professor of Music at Grand Valley State University in Grand Rapids, Michigan. Visit: www.helenmarlais.com

FJH217

TABLE OF CONTENTS

N.B. The key of G♯ minor will be covered in a later book.

A **Minor Scale** is a series of eight tones, starting from the tonic note and ending on the same tonic note one octave higher.

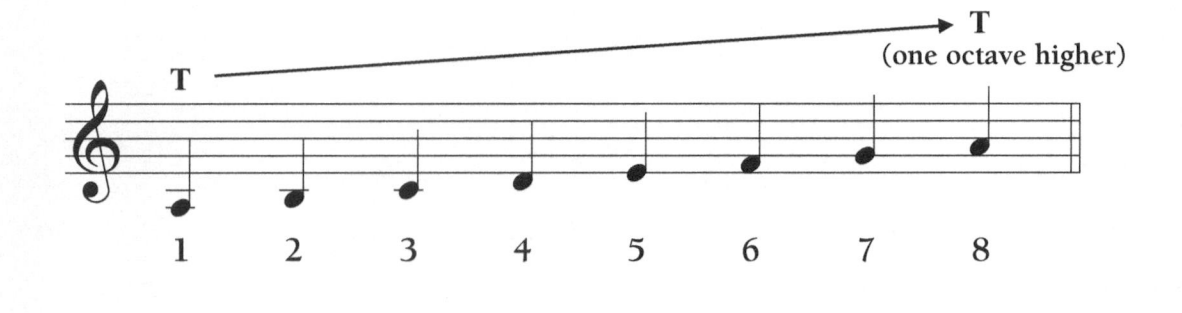

Remember the following pattern to learn and play natural minor scales:

T W H W - W H W W

T = beginning or starting note

W = whole step

H = half step

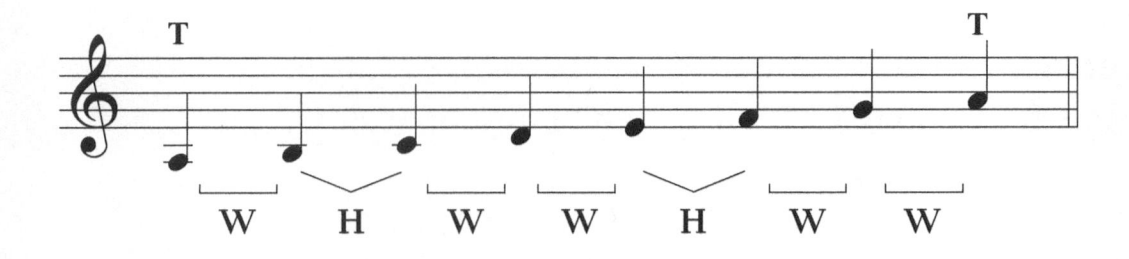

The only half steps in a natural minor scale are between scale degrees **2 and 3** and scale degrees **5 and 6**.

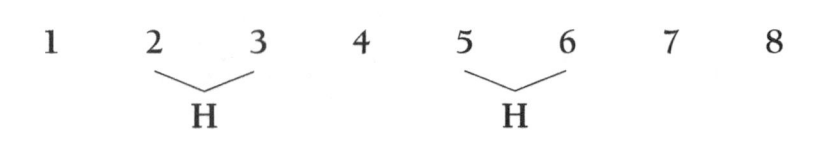

Major and Minor Scales

- When a major scale and a minor scale share the same number of sharps or flats, we say that those two scales are *relatives*.

- *Relative Scales* have exactly the same key signatures, but their starting notes will be different.

- To find the starting note (tonic) of the *relative minor* scale, first look at the key signature of a *major* scale.

  For example: Key of **C Major** (no sharps or flats)

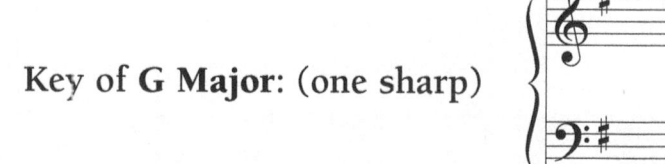

To find the *relative minor* of C Major, move *down* 1½ steps from 'C' to 'A' (*two letter names down*).

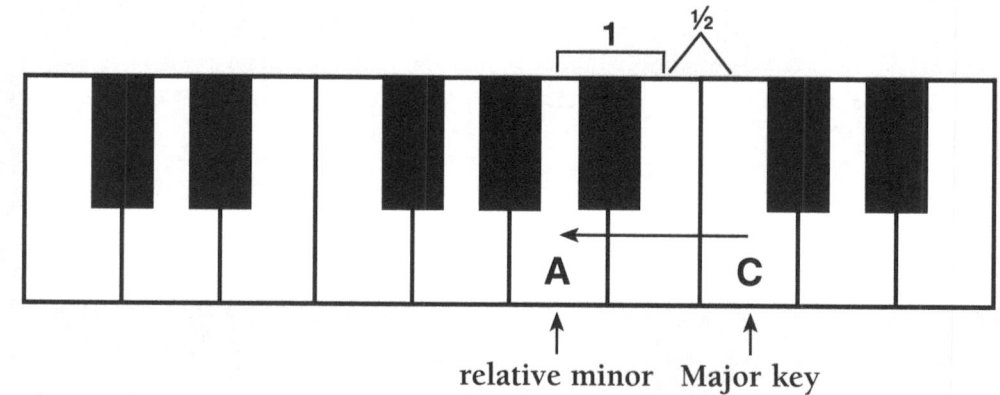

relative minor   Major key

The *relative minor* of C Major is **A minor**, which also has no sharps or flats in its key signature.

Key of **G Major**: (one sharp)

To find the *relative minor* of G Major, move *down* 1½ steps from 'G' to 'E' (*two letter names down*).

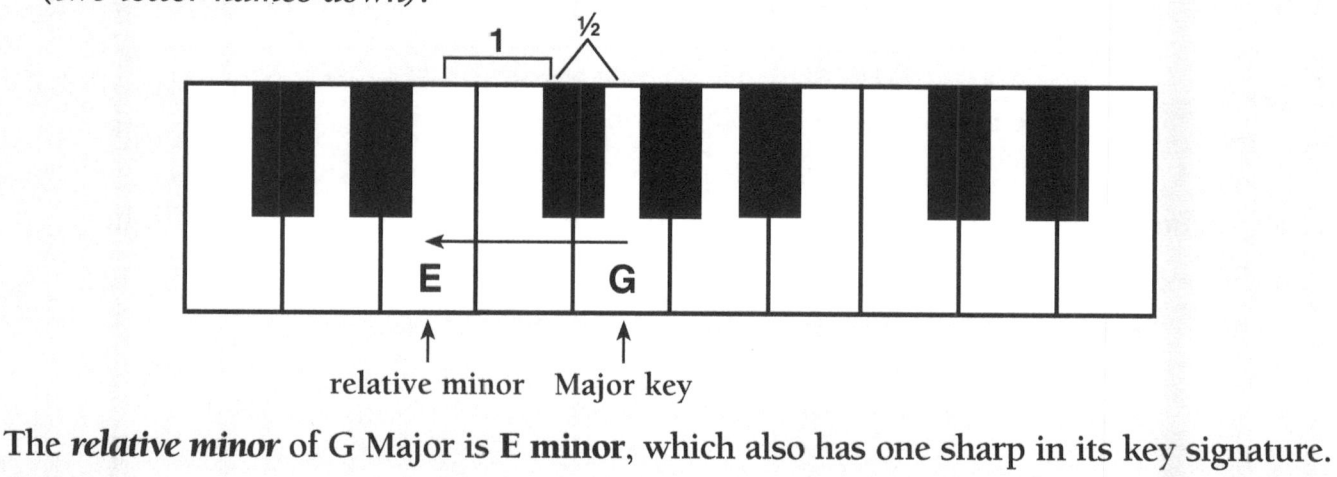

relative minor   Major key

The *relative minor* of G Major is **E minor**, which also has one sharp in its key signature.

Major and Minor Scales

Key of **D Major** (two sharps)

To find the *relative minor* of D Major, move **down** 1½ steps from 'D' to 'B' (*two letter names down*).

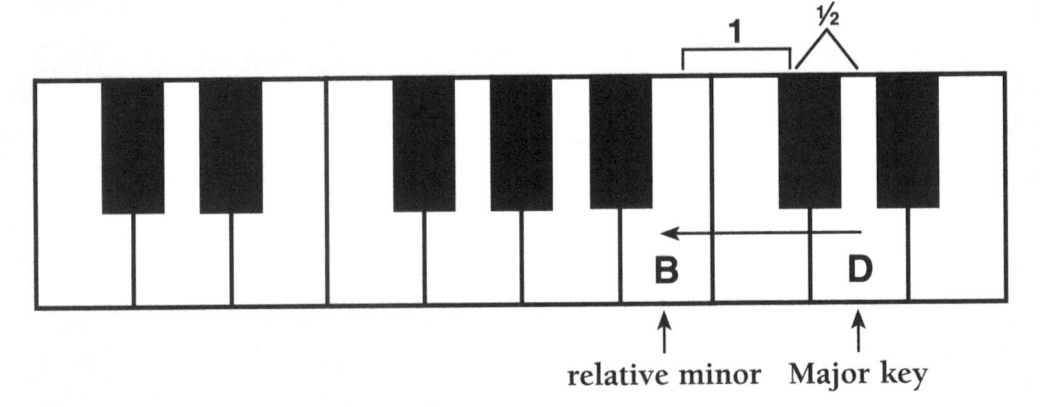

relative minor   Major key

The *relative minor* of D Major is **B minor**, which also has two sharps in its key signature.

Key of **F Major**: (one flat)

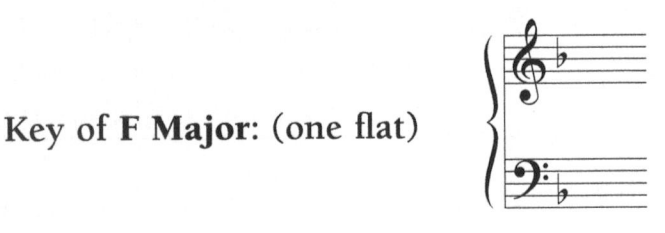

To find the *relative minor* of **F Major**, move **down** 1½ steps from 'F' to 'D' (*two letter names down*).

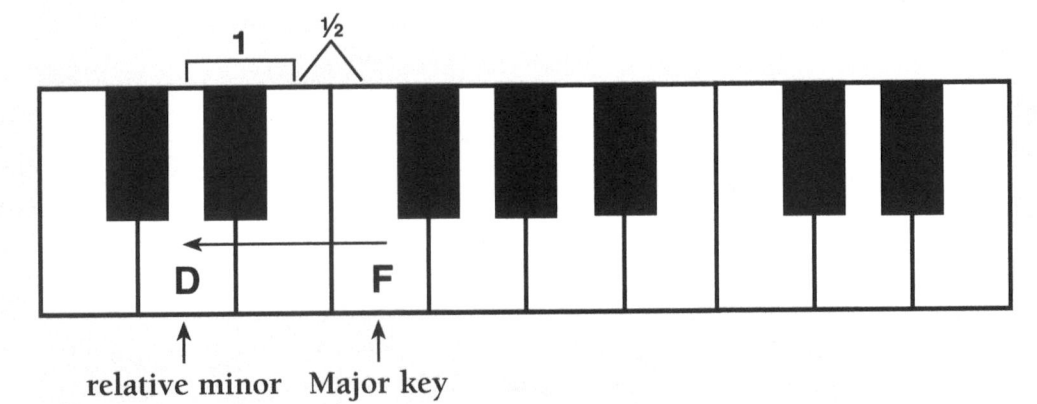

relative minor   Major key

The *relative minor* of F Major is **D minor**, which also has one flat in its key signature.

** To find the *relative Major* of a minor key, move **up** 1½ steps.**

FJH2175

Minor Cadences

This cadence is made up of **i** (tonic) and **iv** (subdominant),
and **V⁷** (dominant seventh) chords.

A minor cadence:

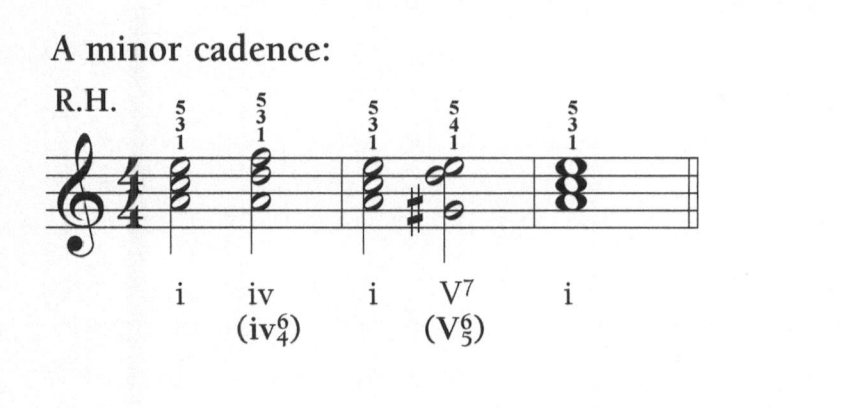

Focus on the **iv** chord:

Look at the iv chord. It is made up of an interval of a 4th and an interval of a 6th.
This is why this form of the iv chord is called the iv⁶ chord.

Now focus on the **V⁷** chord:

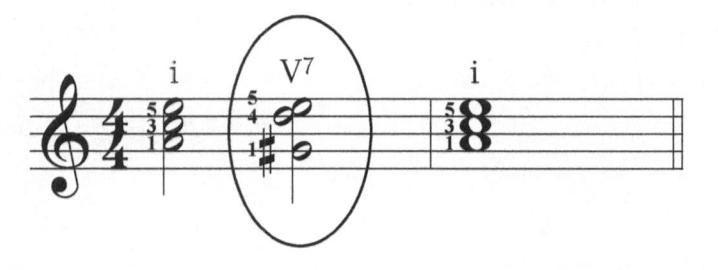

The **V⁷** chord is made up of an interval of a 5th and an interval of a 6th:

For that reason, this form of the **V⁷** chord is called the V⁶ chord.

Play the cadence at the top of this page (both hands)
and think about the intervals.

Note to Teachers: This cadence is called an **Authentic cadence,** because it
ends in V⁷-i. Authentic cadences close with some form of V-i or V⁷-i.

Key of A Minor

key signature: no sharps or flats

relative major key: C Major

Mark the two half steps on this keyboard:

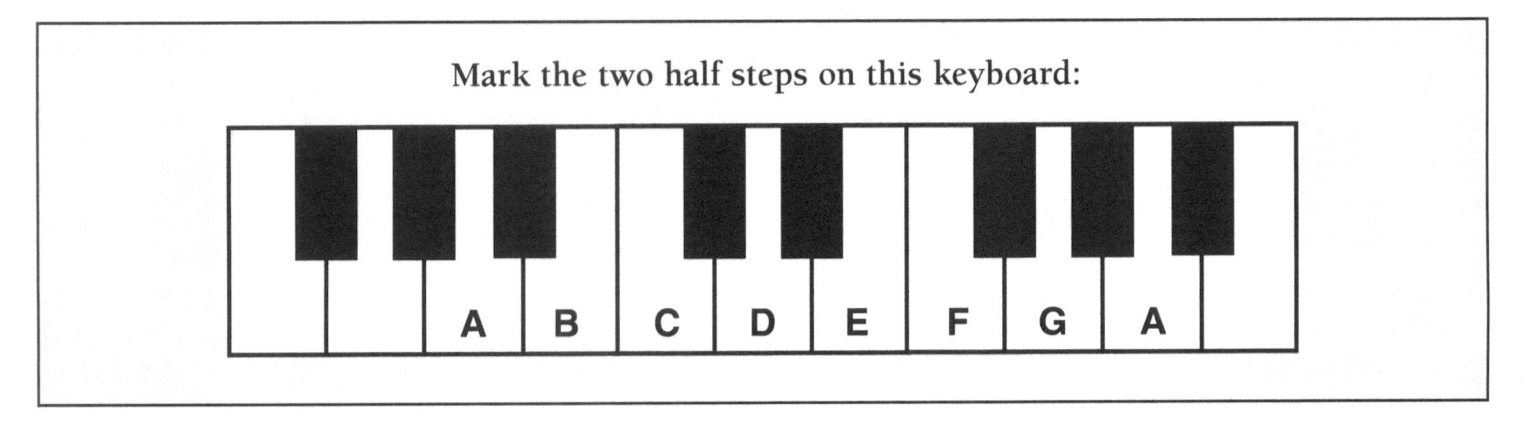

A B C D E F G A

A Natural Minor One-Octave Scale and Cadence

i   iv   i   V⁷   i
(iv⁶₄)   (V⁶₅)

One-Octave A Minor Arpeggio

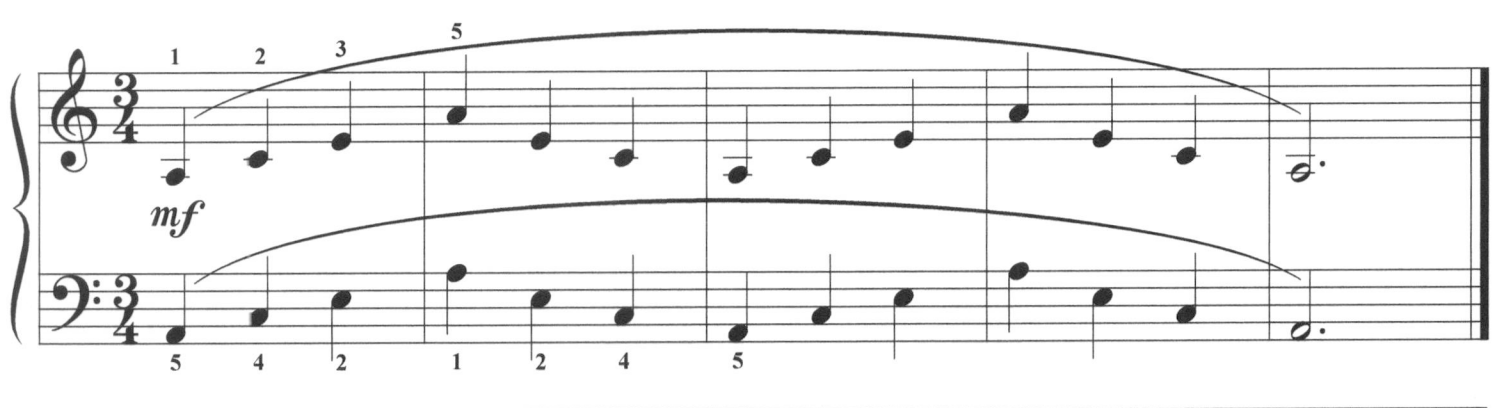

Note to the Teacher: This book covers only the natural form of the minor scale (the minor scales that follow their key signatures exactly). However, in order to produce cadences that end with a correctly spelled dominant-seventh chord (V7) it is necessary to raise the seventh scale degree from the key signature. For example, G-sharp rather than G-natural in the A minor cadence pattern. The cadence patterns for all minor keys in Book 3 will employ the raised seventh scale degree.

Key of E Minor

key signature: one sharp – (F♯)
relative major key: G Major

Mark the two half steps on this keyboard:

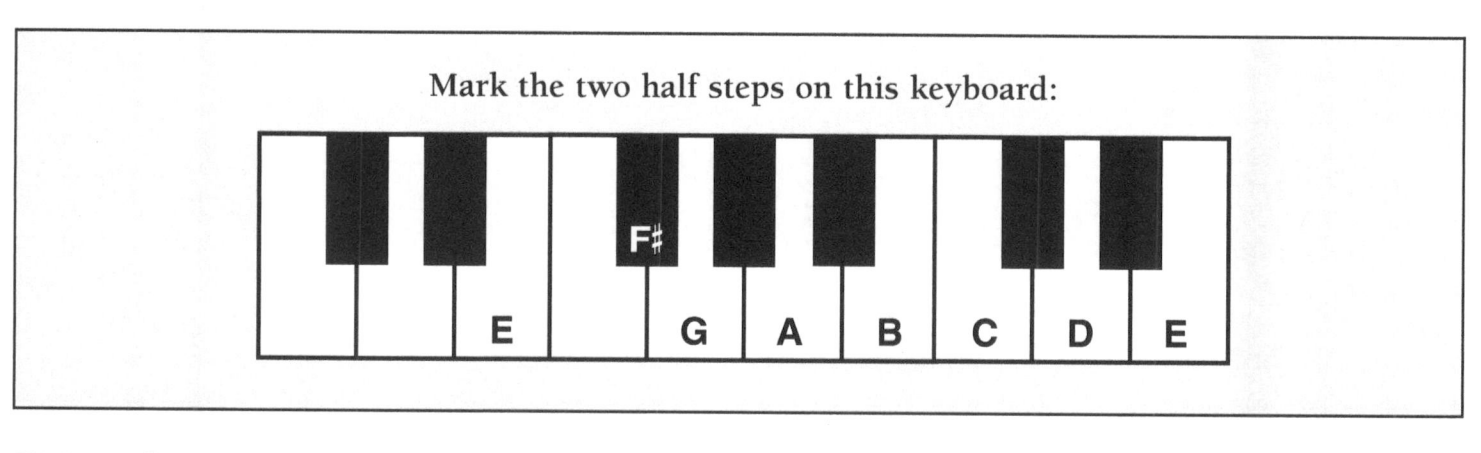

E Natural Minor One-Octave Scale and Cadence

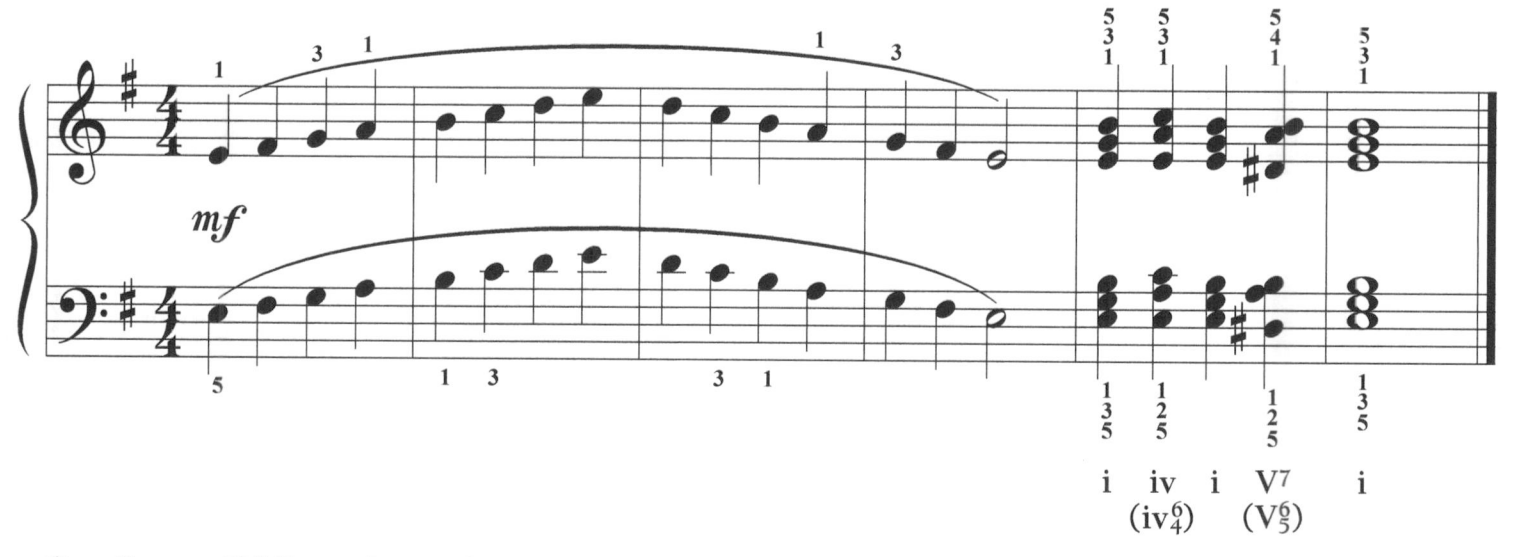

i   iv   i   V⁷   i
(iv⁶₄)   (V⁶₅)

One-Octave E Minor Arpeggio

Key of D Minor

key signature: one flat – (B♭)
relative major key: F Major

Mark the two half steps on this keyboard:

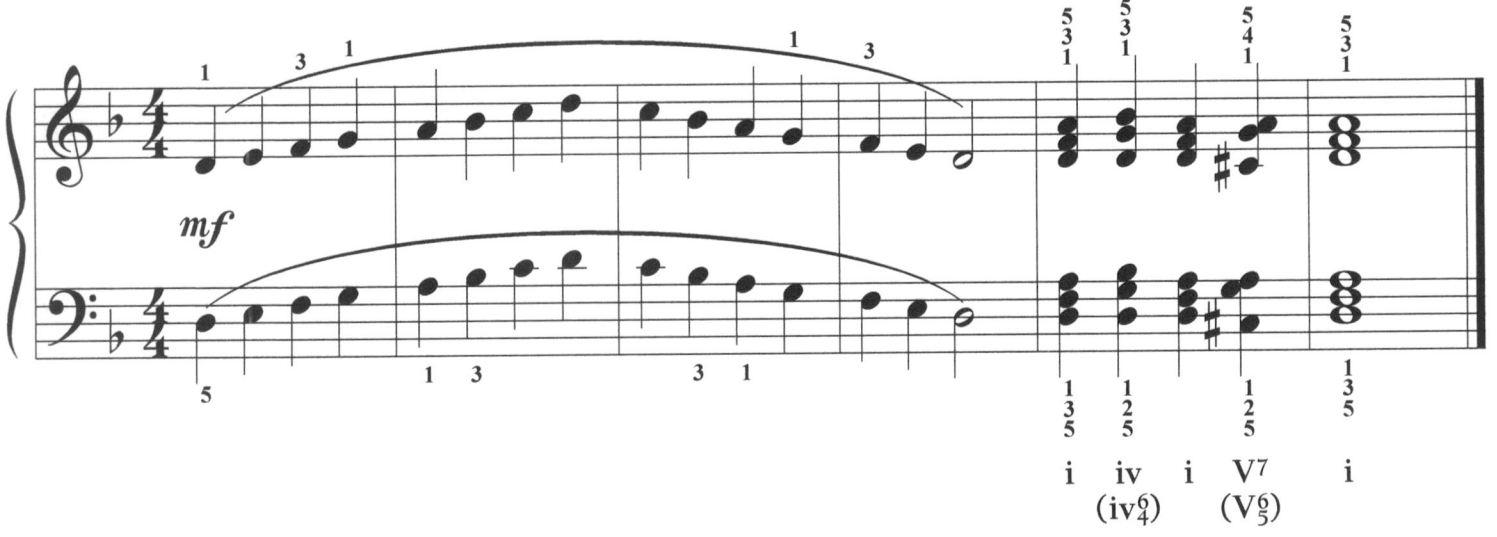

D E F G A C D

D Natural Minor One-Octave Scale and Cadence

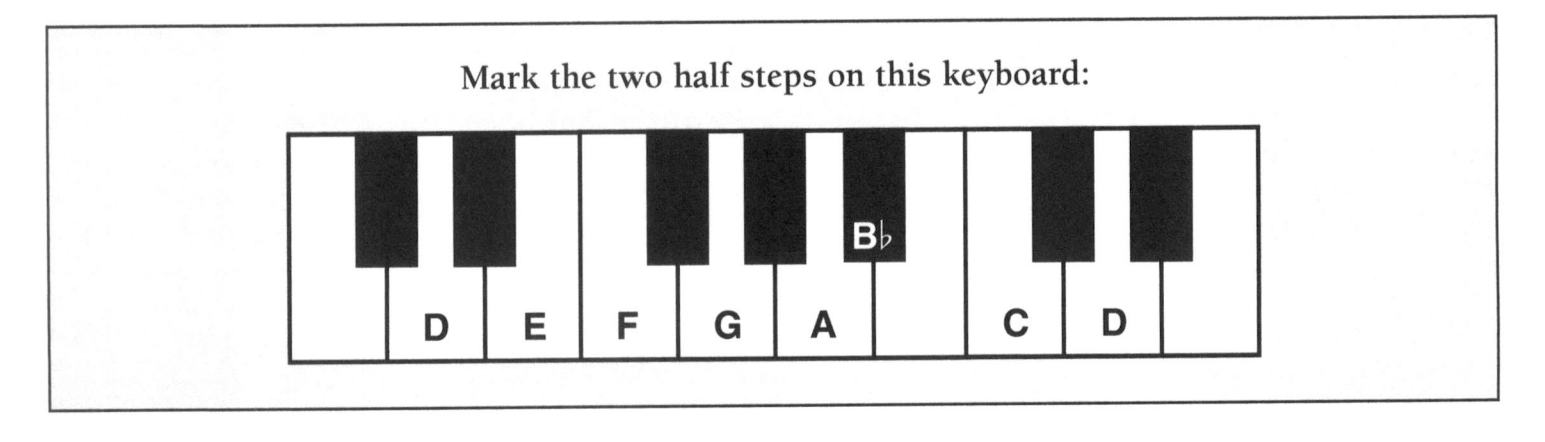

i   iv   i   V⁷   i
   (iv⁶₄)   (V⁶₅)

One-Octave D Minor Arpeggio

FJH2175

Key of G Minor

key signature: two flats – (B♭, E♭)
relative major key: B♭ Major

Mark the two half steps on this keyboard:

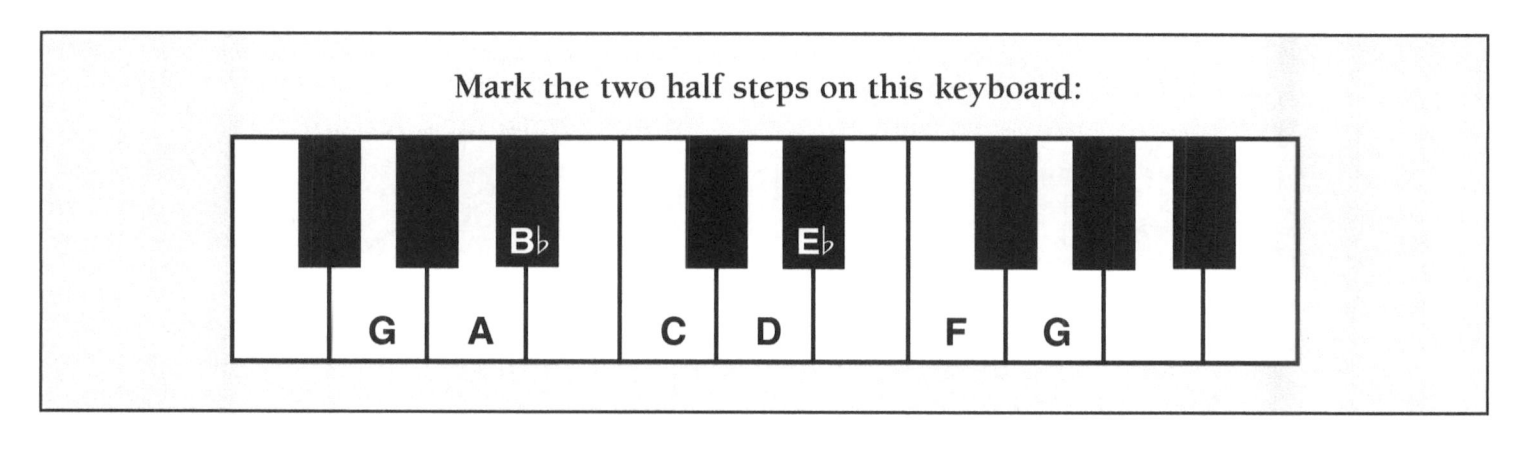

G Natural Minor One-Octave Scale and Cadence

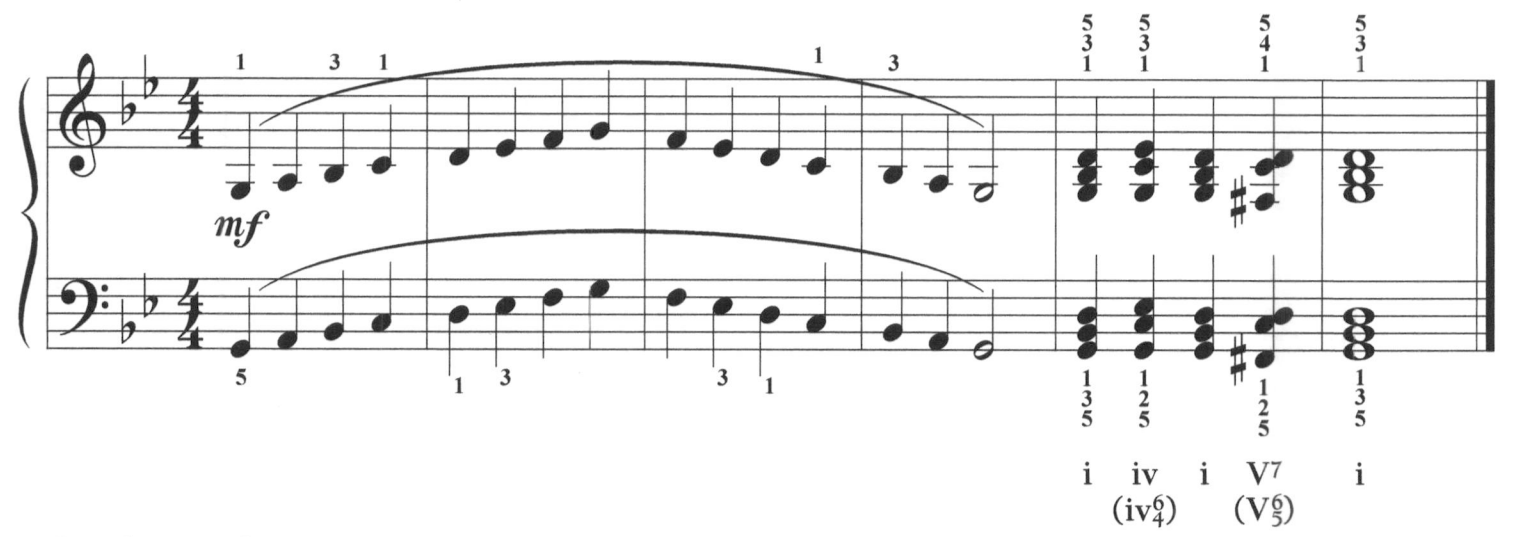

i   iv   i   V⁷   i
(iv⁶₄)   (V⁶₅)

One-Octave G Minor Arpeggio

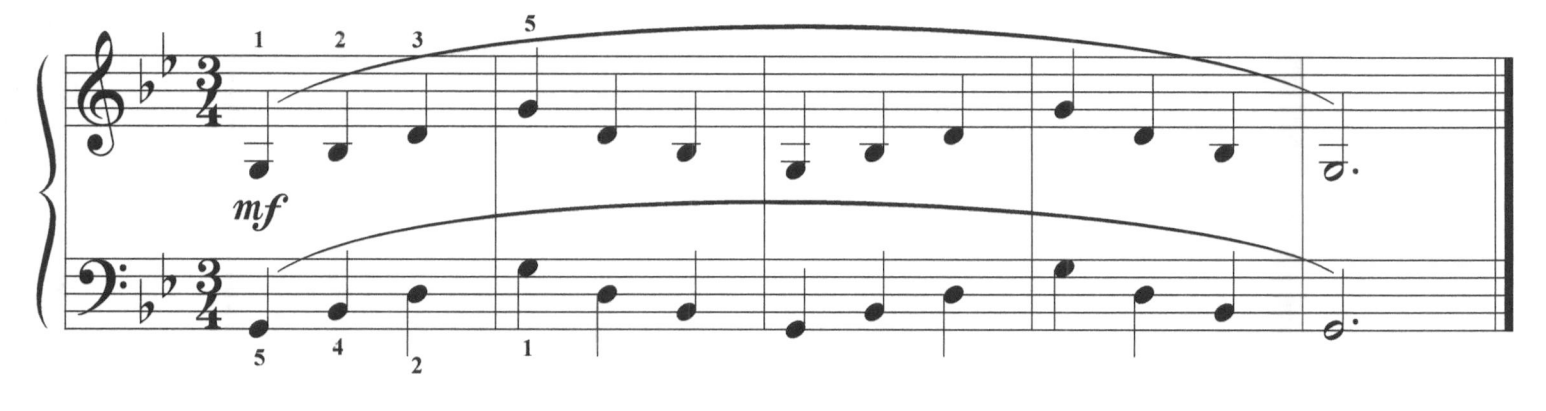

Key of C Minor

key signature: three flats – (B♭, E♭, A♭)
relative major key: E♭ Major

Mark the two half steps on this keyboard:

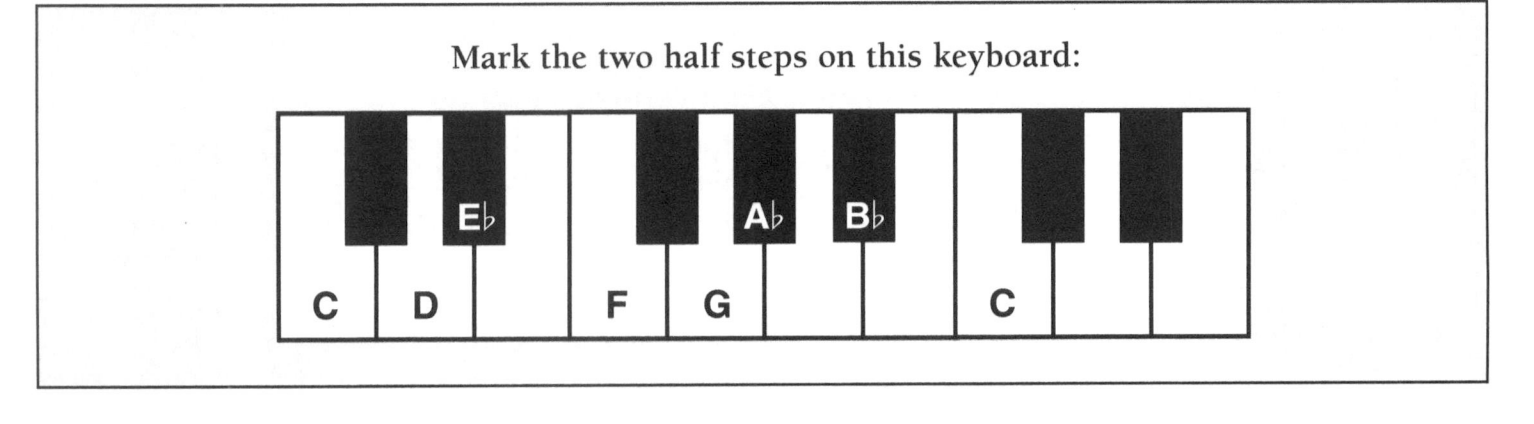

C Natural Minor One-Octave Scale and Cadence

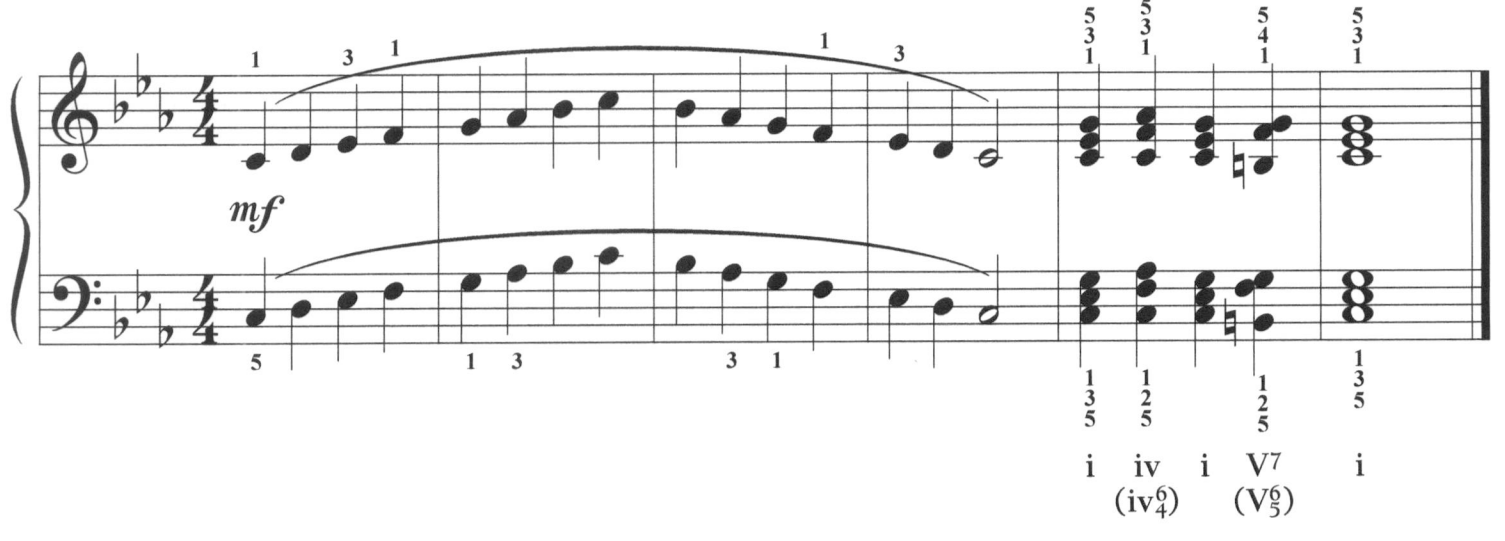

i   iv   i   V⁷   i
(iv⁶₄)   (V⁶₅)

One-Octave C Minor Arpeggio

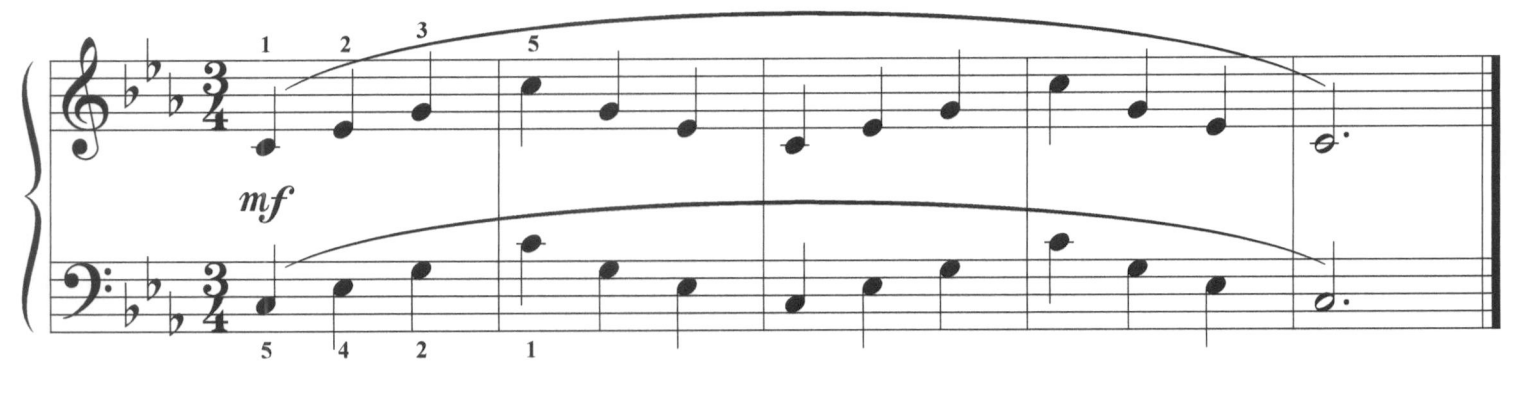

FJH2175

Key of B Minor

key signature: two sharps – (F♯, C♯)
relative major key: D Major

Mark the two half steps on this keyboard:

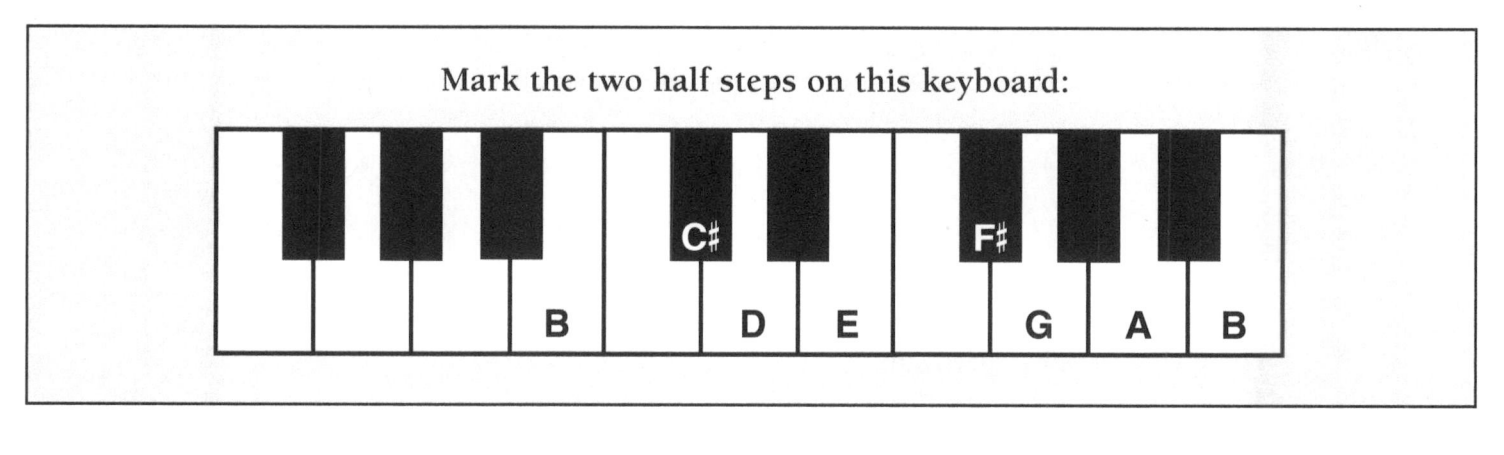

B Natural Minor One-Octave Scale and Cadence

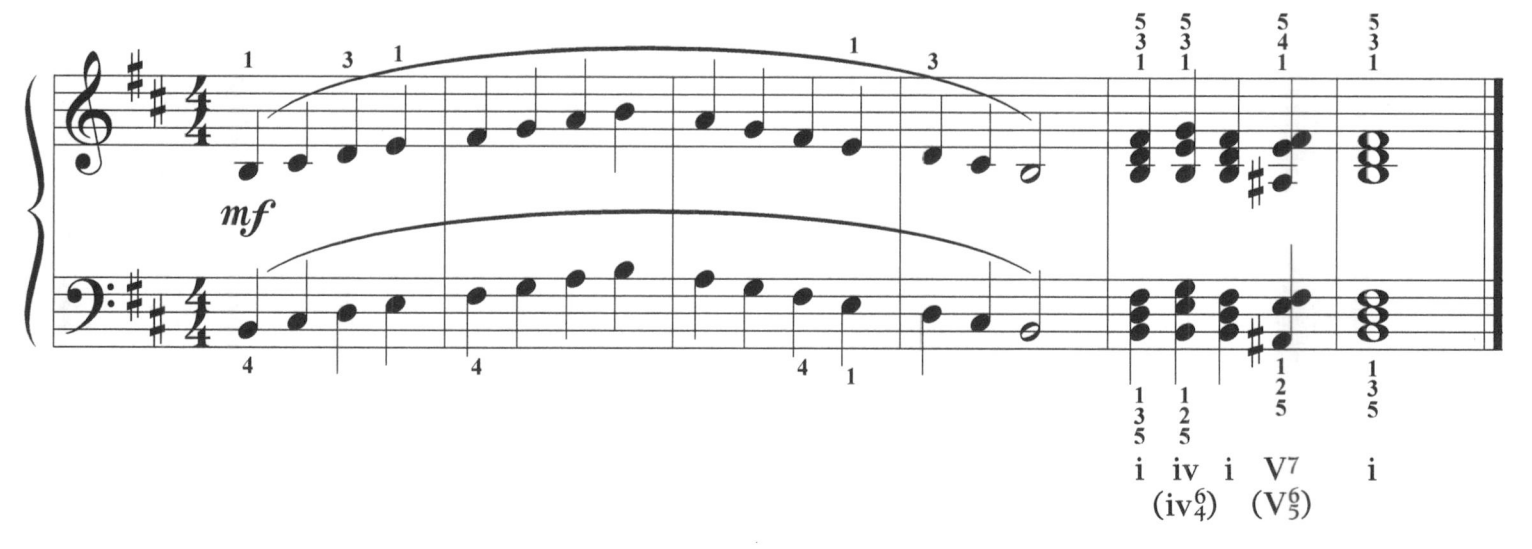

i   iv   i   V⁷   i
(iv⁶₄) (V⁶₅)

One-Octave B Minor Arpeggio

FJH2175

13

Key of F Minor

key signature: four flats – (B♭, E♭, A♭, D♭)
relative major key: A♭ Major

Mark the two half steps on this keyboard:

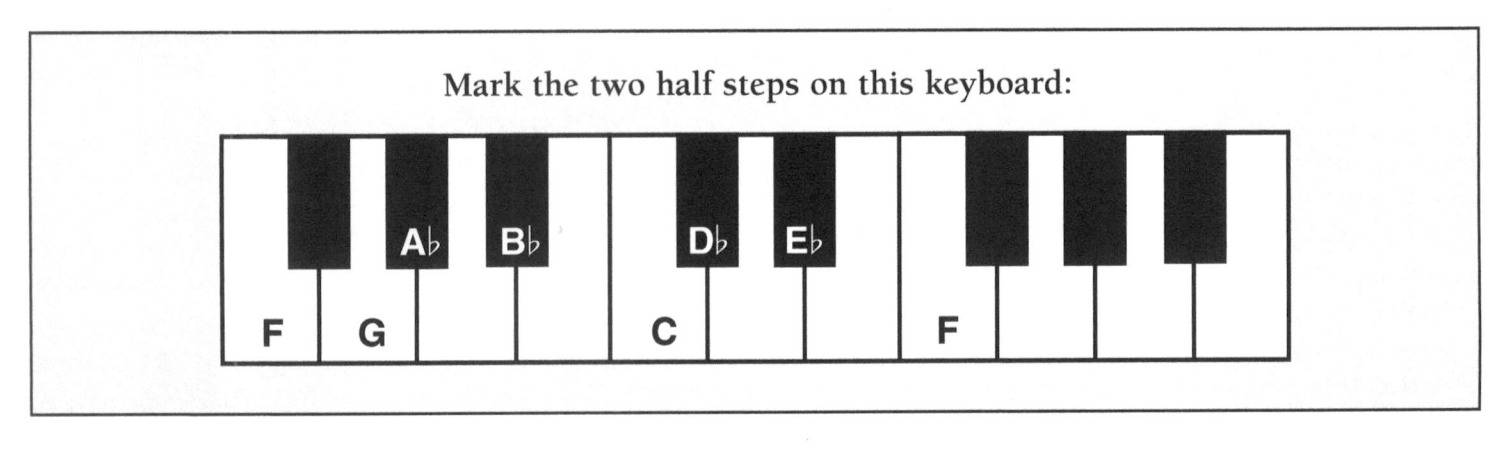

F Natural Minor One-Octave Scale and Cadence

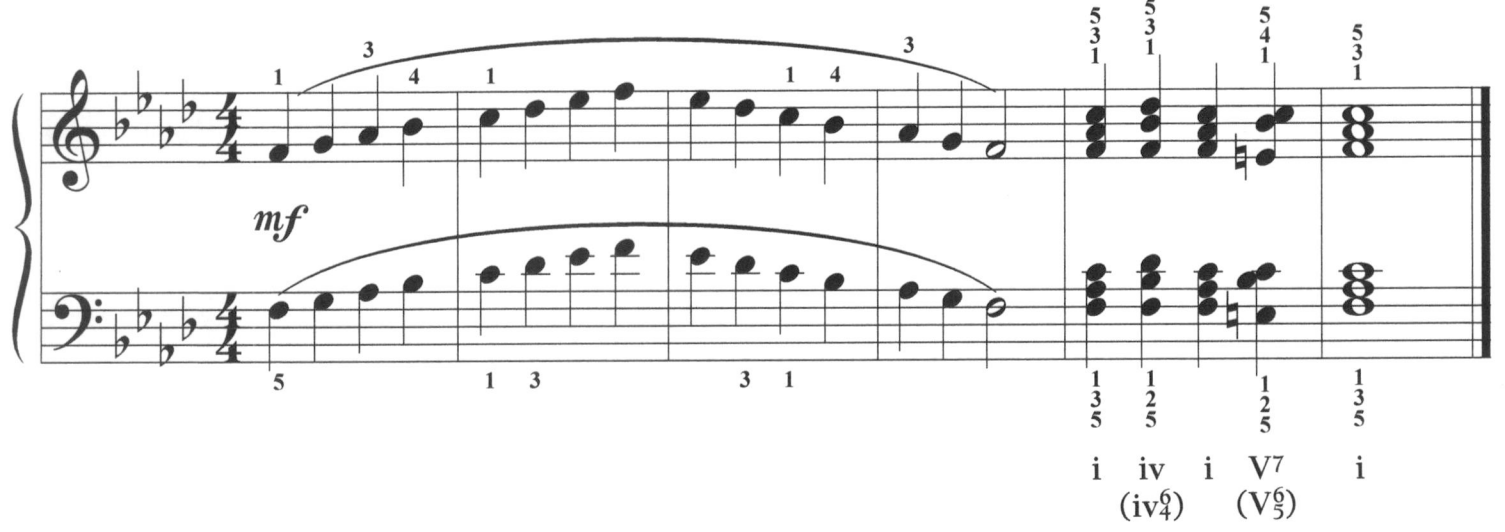

i   iv   i   V⁷   i
(iv⁶₄)   (V⁶₅)

One-Octave F Minor Arpeggio

Key of B♭ Minor

key signature: five flats – (B♭, E♭, A♭, D♭, G♭)
relative major key: D♭ Major

Mark the two half steps on this keyboard:

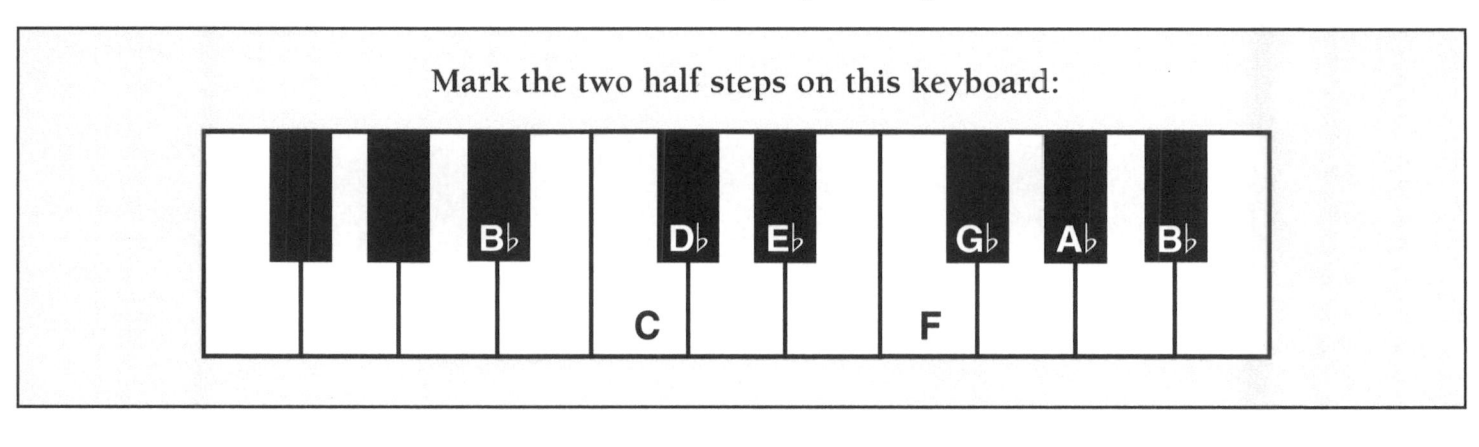

B♭ Natural Minor One-Octave Scale and Cadence

i   iv   i   V⁷   i
     (iv⁶₄)   (V⁶₅)

One-Octave B♭ Minor Arpeggio

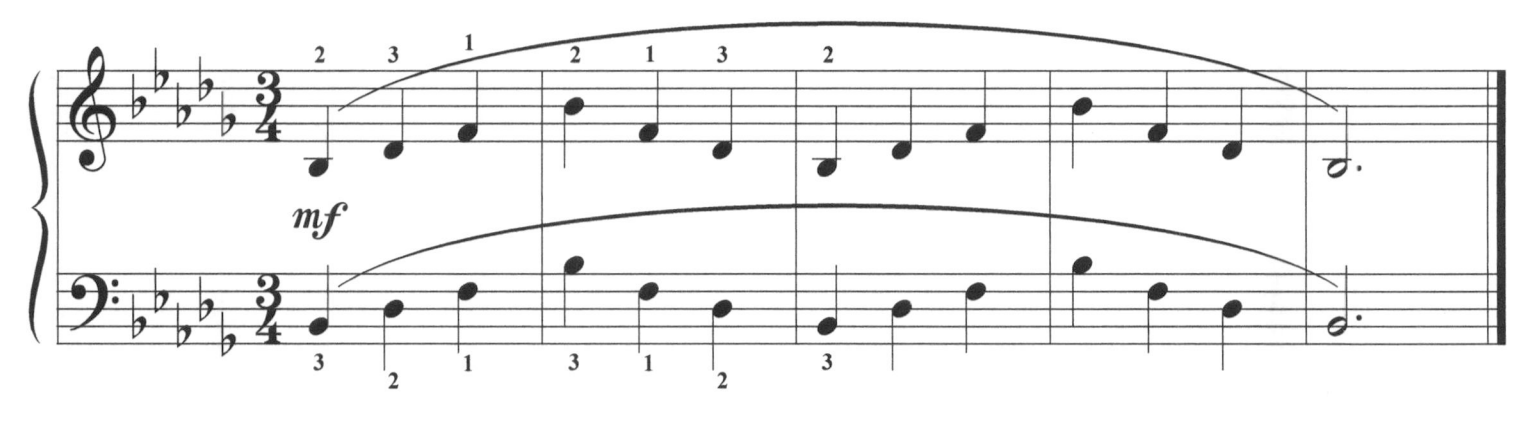

Key of E♭ Minor

key signature: six flats – (B♭, E♭, A♭, D♭, G♭, C♭)
relative major key: G♭ Major

Mark the two half steps on this keyboard:

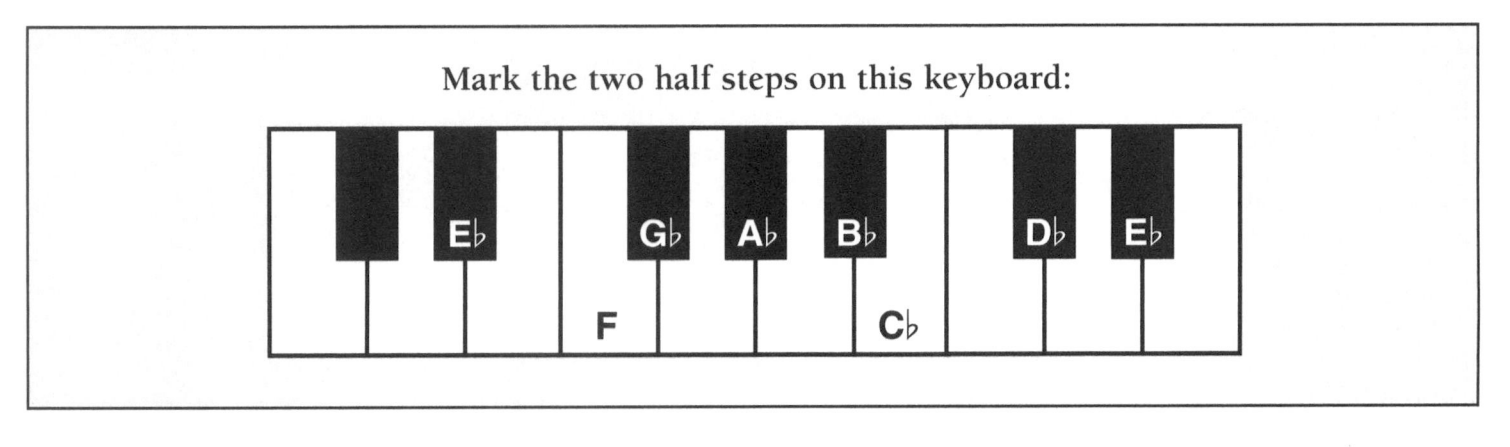

E♭ Natural Minor One-Octave Scale and Cadence

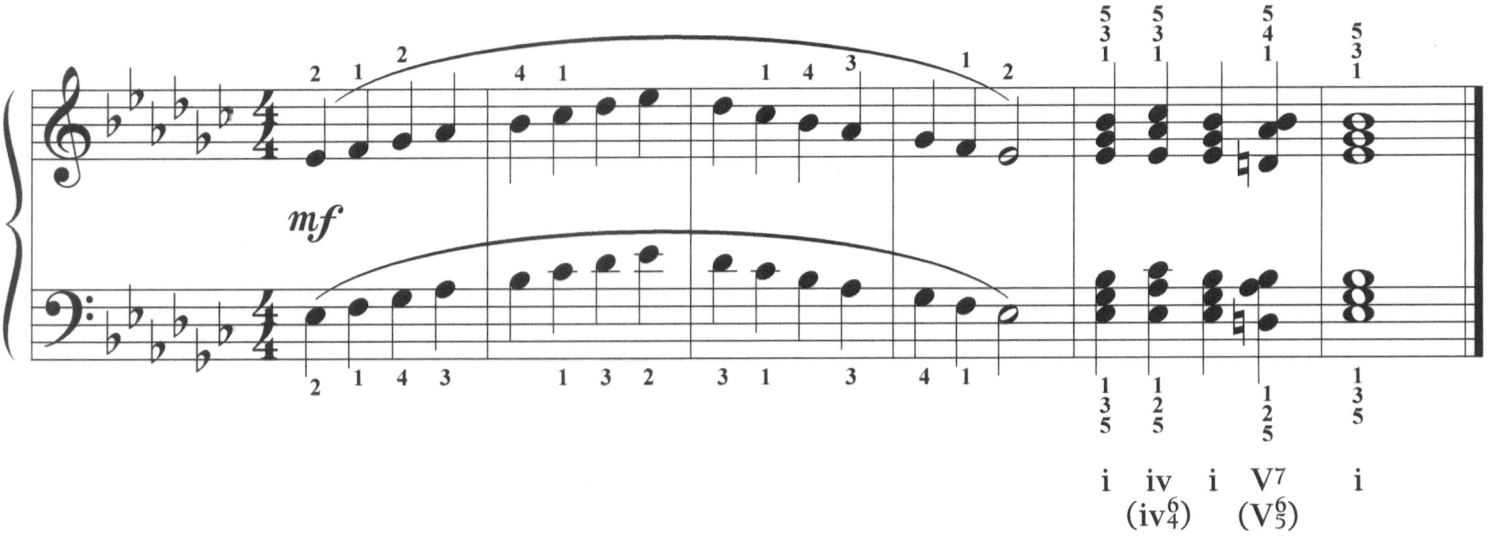

i   iv   i   V⁷   i
(iv⁶₄)   (V⁶₅)

One-Octave E♭ Minor Arpeggio

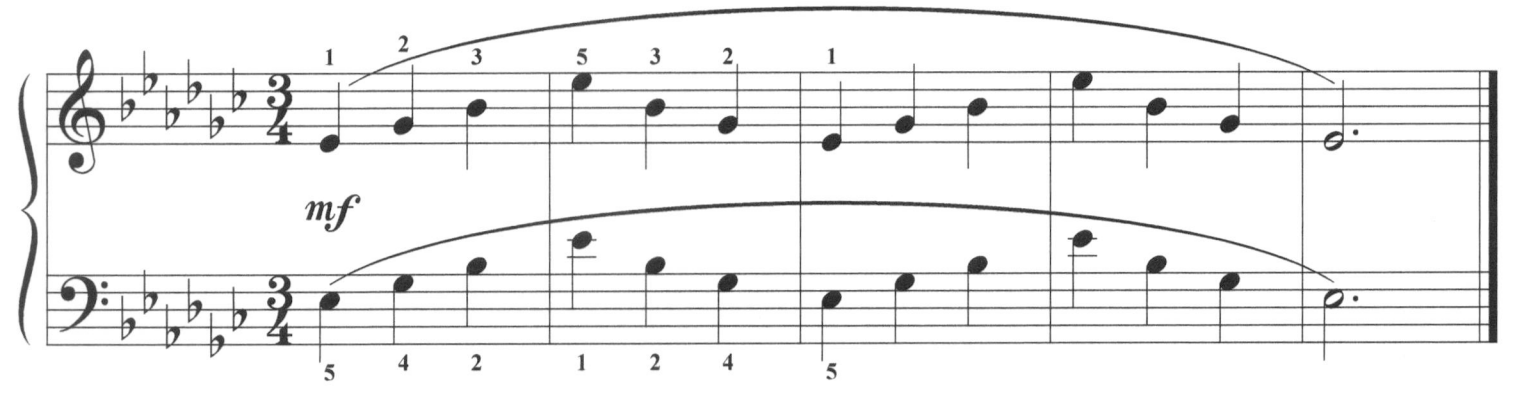

16

Key of A♭ Minor

key signature: seven flats – (B♭, E♭, A♭, D♭, G♭, C♭, F♭)
relative major key: C♭ Major

Mark the two half steps on this keyboard:

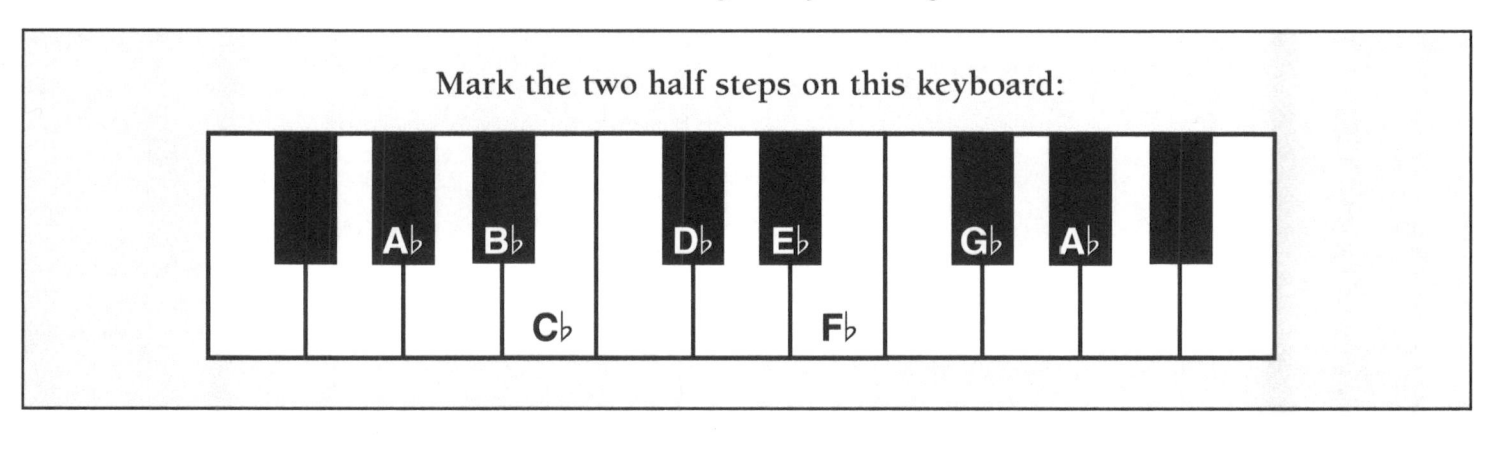

A♭ Natural Minor One-Octave Scale and Cadence

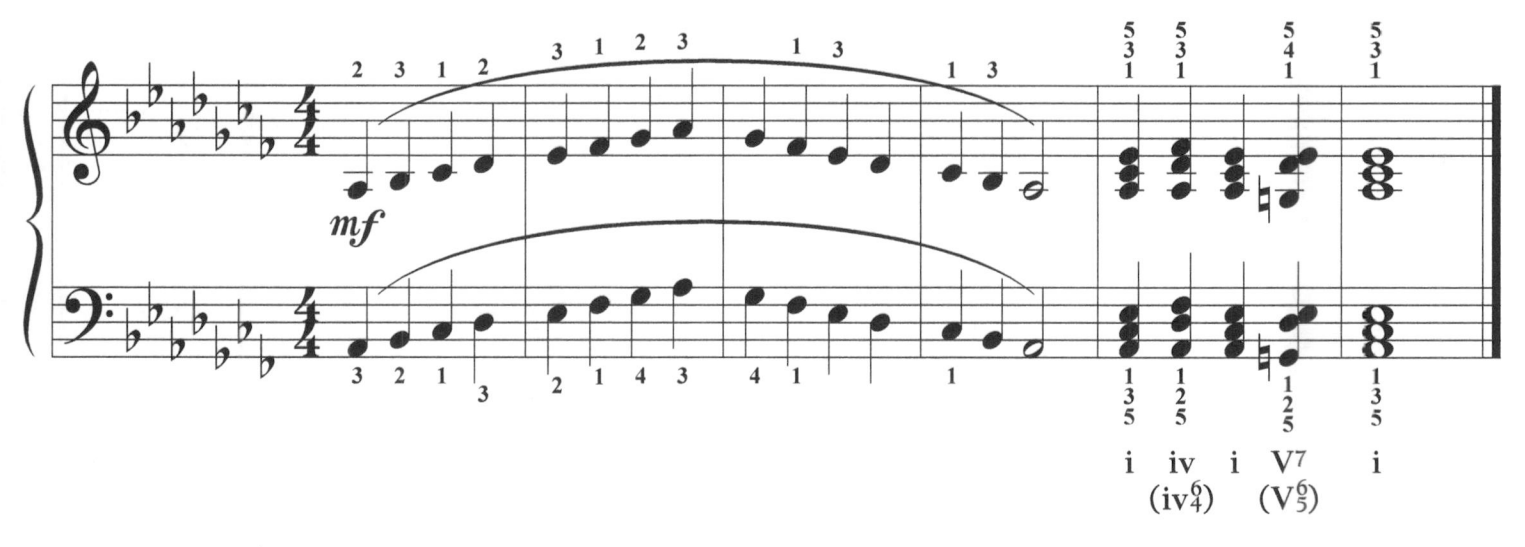

One-Octave A♭ Minor Arpeggio

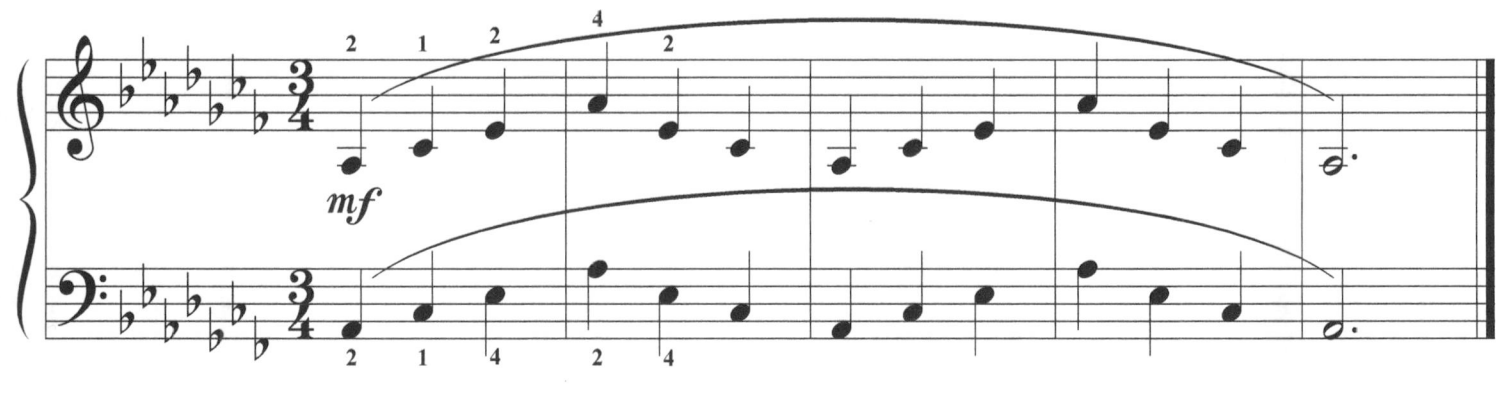

Key of F# Minor

key signature: three sharps – (F#, C#, G#)
relative major key: A Major

Mark the two half steps on this keyboard:

F# G# C# F#
A B D E

F# Natural Minor One-Octave Scale and Cadence

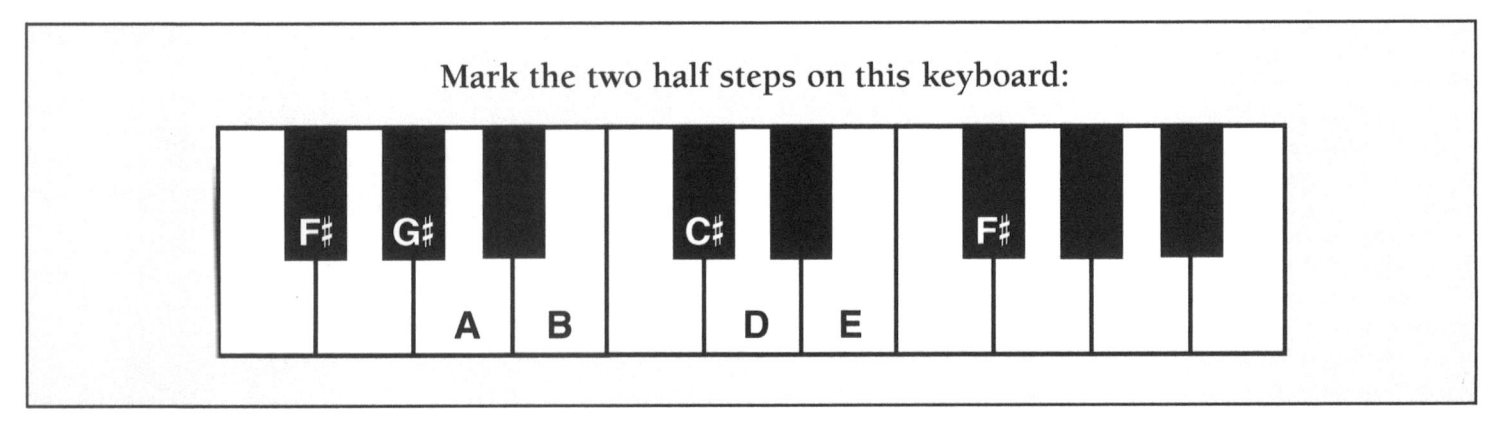

i iv i V⁷ i
(iv⁶₄) (V⁶₅)

One-Octave F# Minor Arpeggio

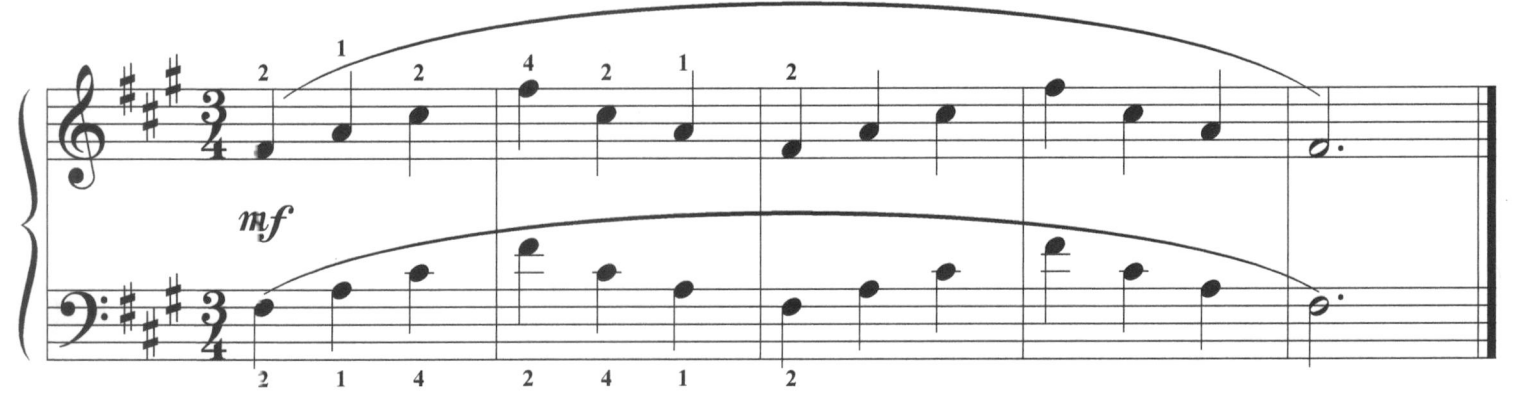

18

FJH2175

Key of C# Minor

key signature: four sharps – (F#, C#, G#, D#)
relative major key: E Major

Mark the two half steps on this keyboard:

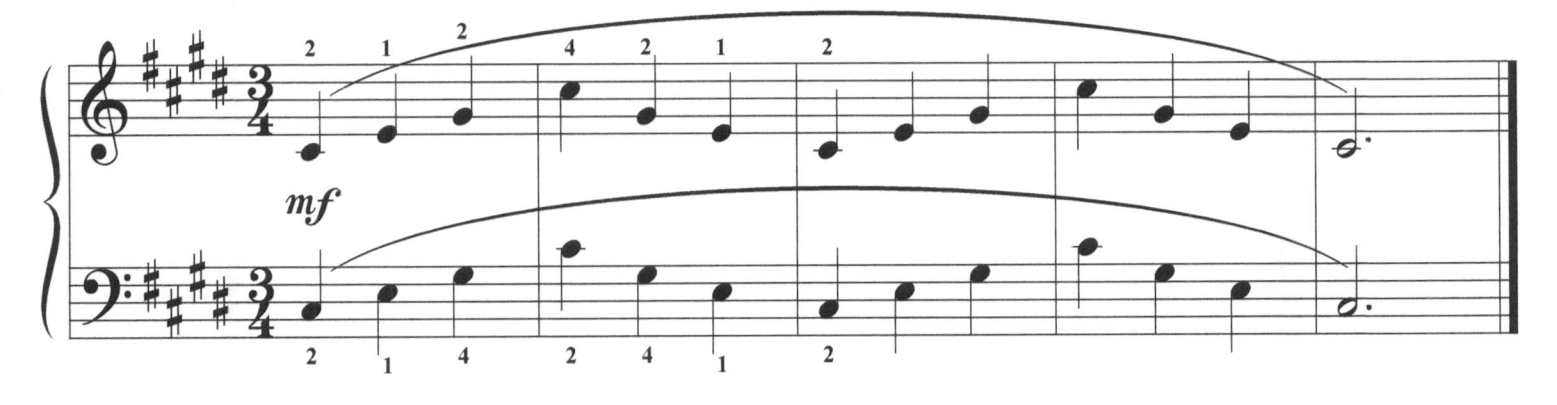

C# Natural Minor One-Octave Scale and Cadence

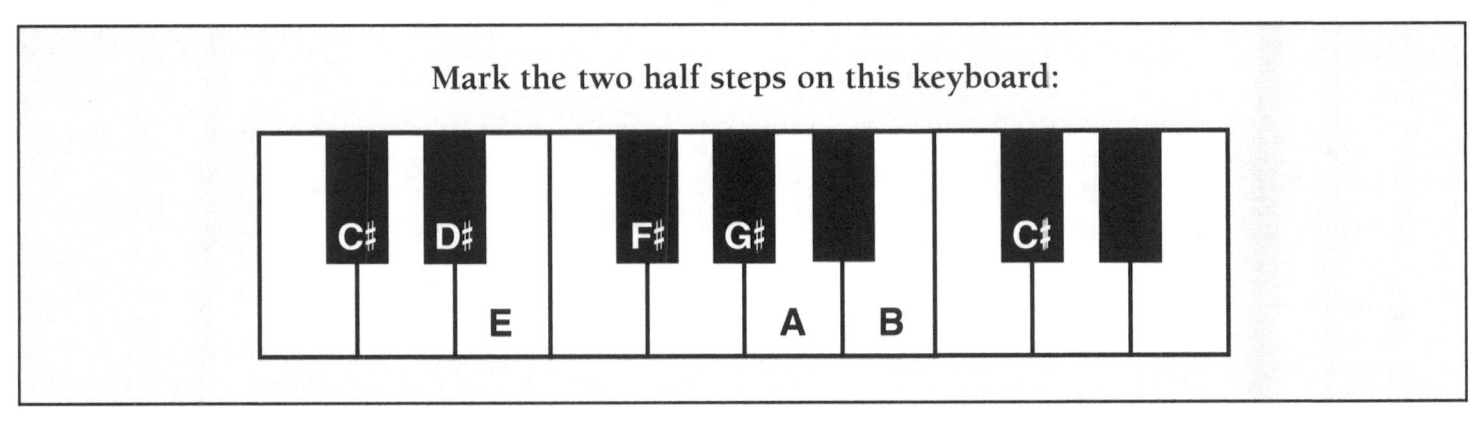

i iv i V⁷ i
(iv⁶₄) (V⁶₅)

One-Octave C# Minor Arpeggio

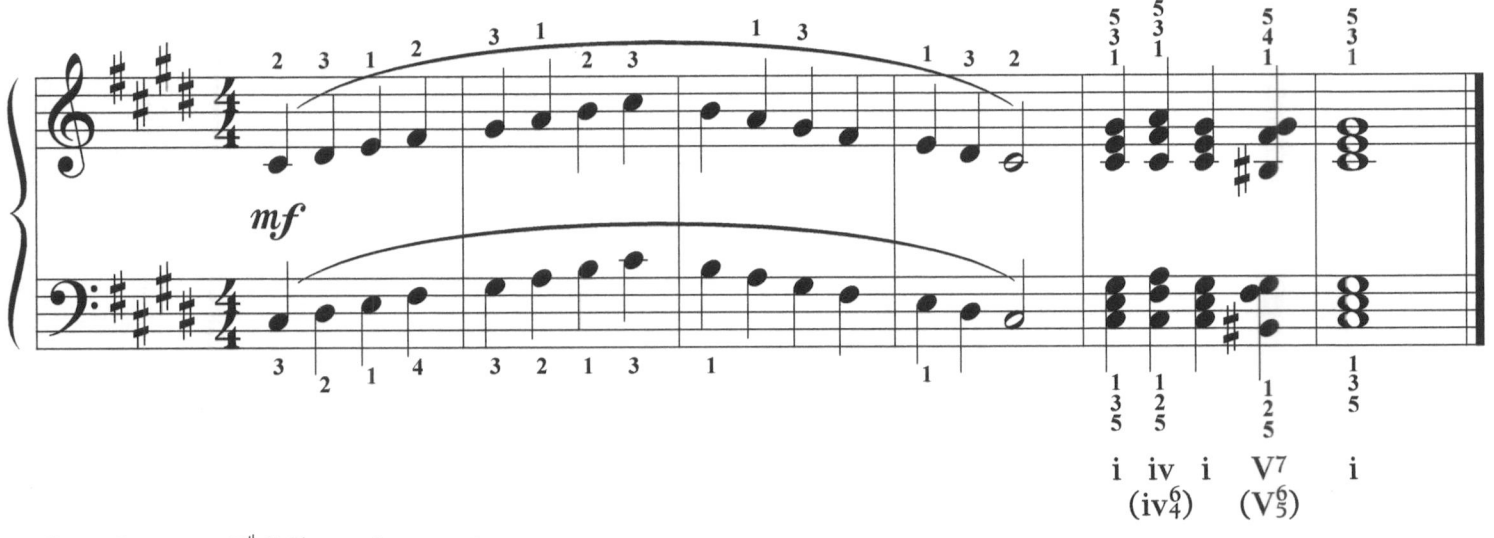

Key of D# Minor

key signature: six sharps – (F#, C#, G#, D#, A#, E#)
relative major key: F# Major

Mark the two half steps on this keyboard:

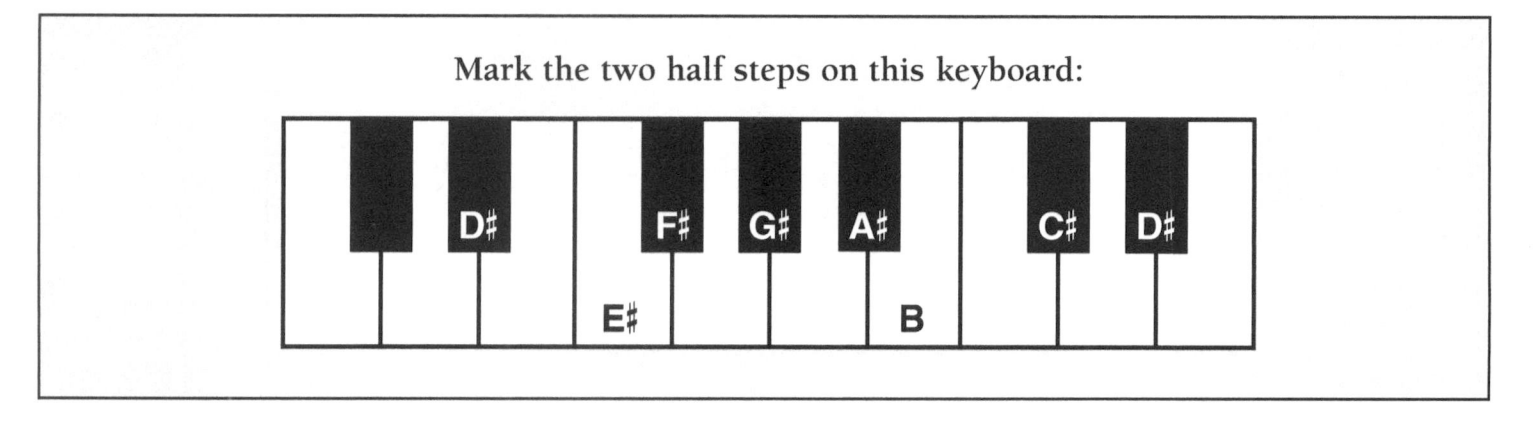

D# Natural Minor One-Octave Scale and Cadence

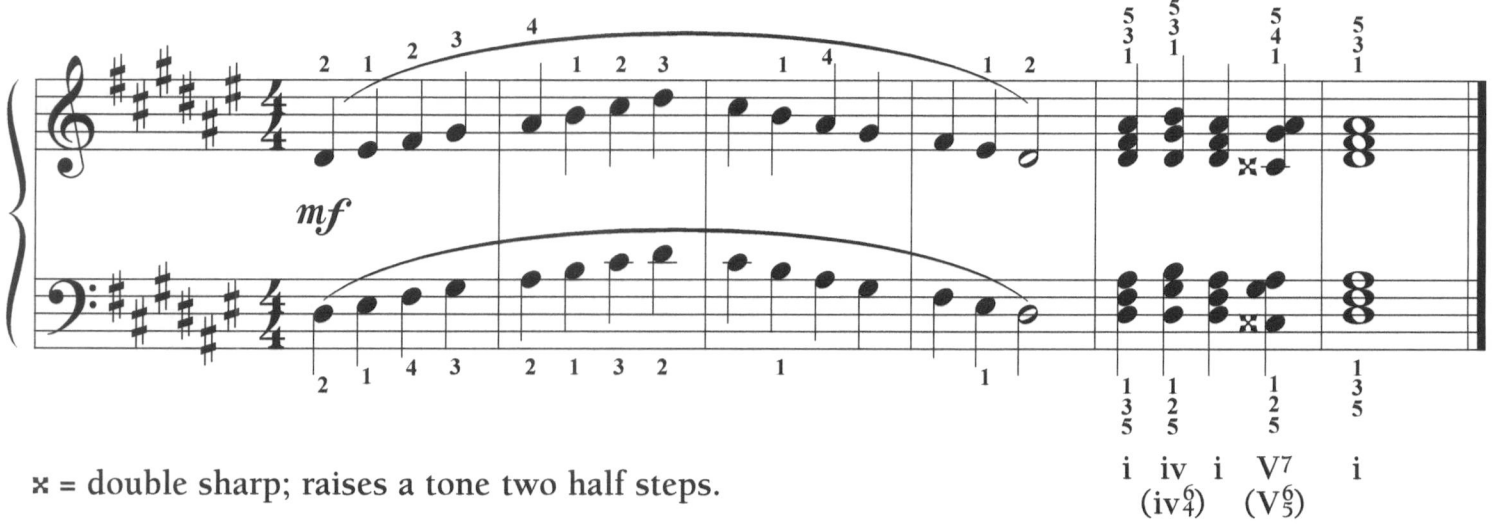

i   iv   i   V7   i
(iv⁶₄)   (V⁶₅)

✗ = double sharp; raises a tone two half steps.

One-Octave D# Minor Arpeggio

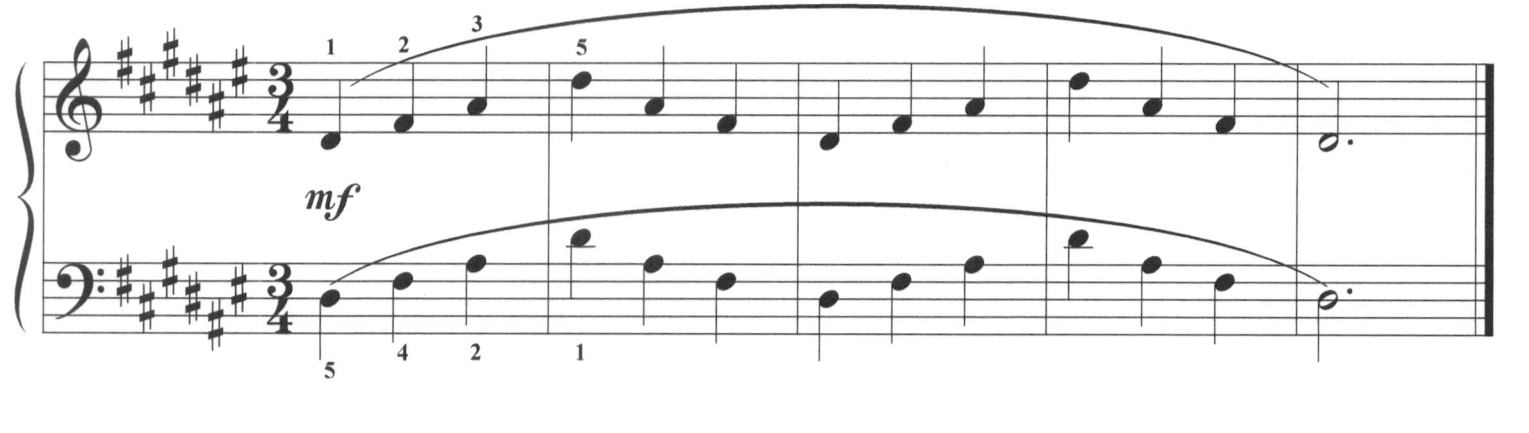

FJH2175

Key of A♯ Minor

key signature: seven sharps – (F♯, C♯, G♯, D♯, A♯, E♯, B♯)
relative major key: C♯ Major

Mark the two half steps on this keyboard:

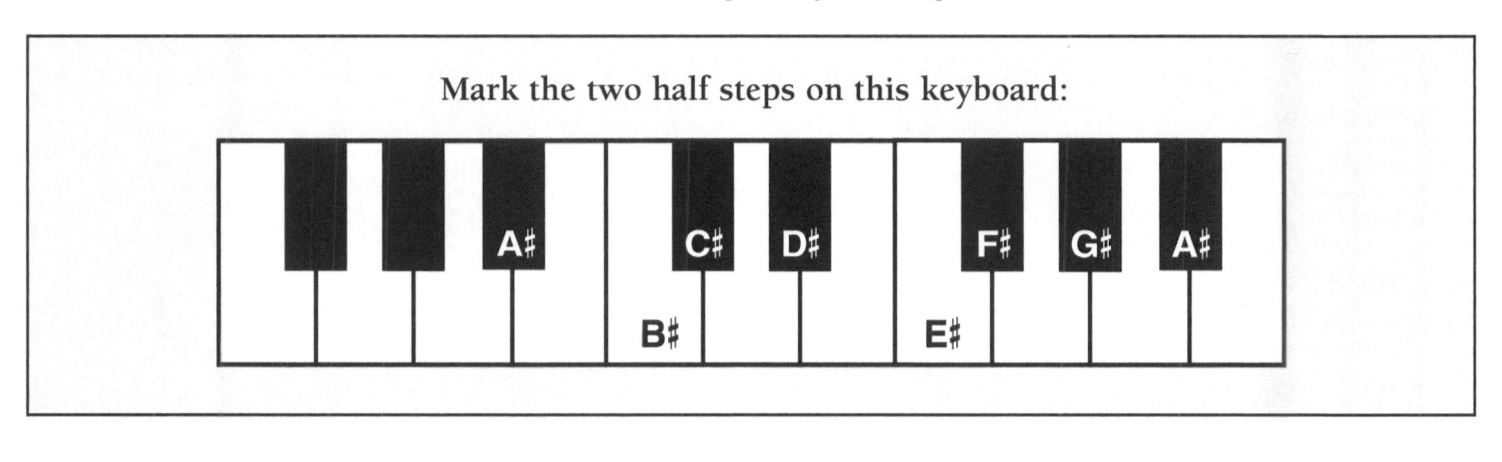

A♯ Natural Minor One-Octave Scale and Cadence

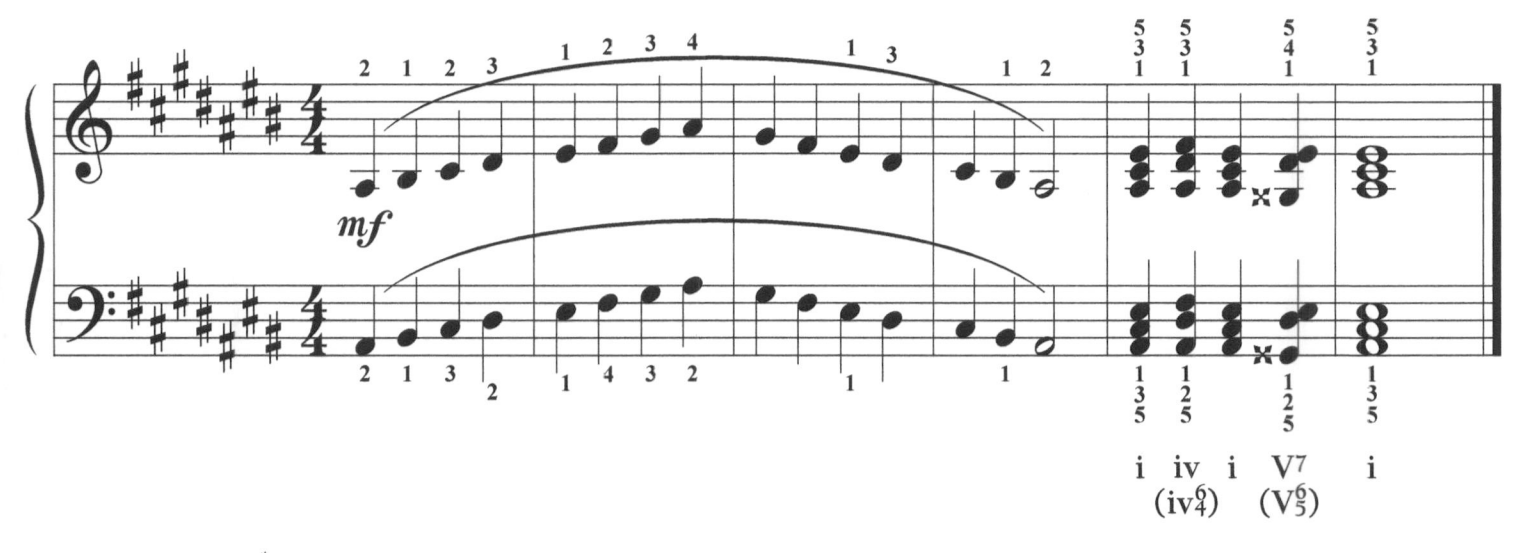

i   iv   i   V⁷   i
(iv$_4^6$)   (V$_3^6$)

One-Octave A♯ Minor Arpeggio

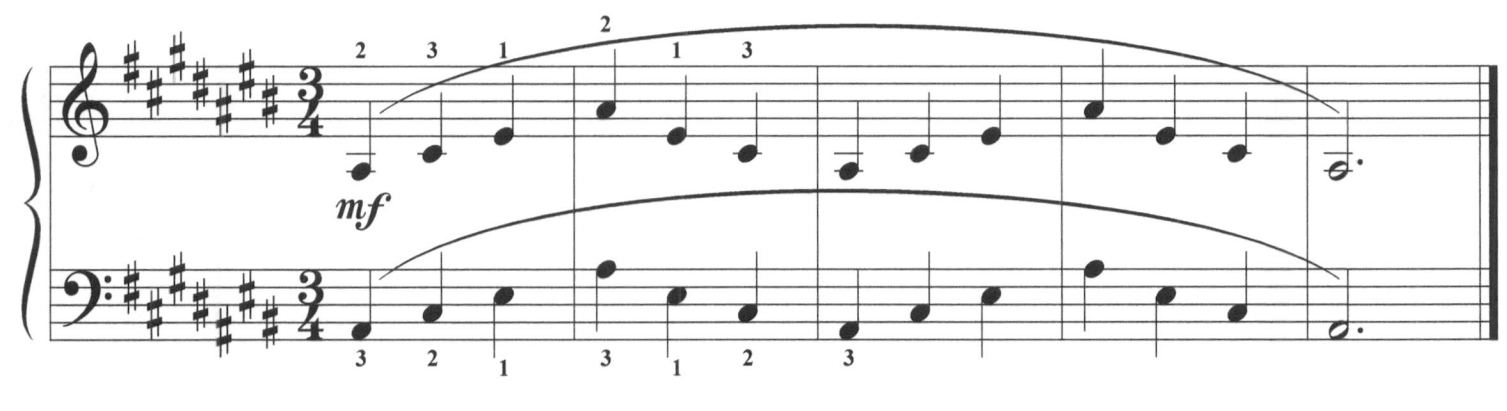

Fingering Charts for Natural Minor Scales

□ = white keys   ▲ = black keys

All fingerings in these charts are written for ascending scales.
(Read backwards to play the descending scales.)

Group No. 1—A minor, E minor, D minor, G minor, and C minor
Scales that have the *same fingering*

- Notice that the **third fingers** of both hands are always played at the same time.†
- Notice that the **first and second fingers** of both hands are played together in the middle of the scale, but the second finger in one hand plays at the same time as the first finger in the other hand.*

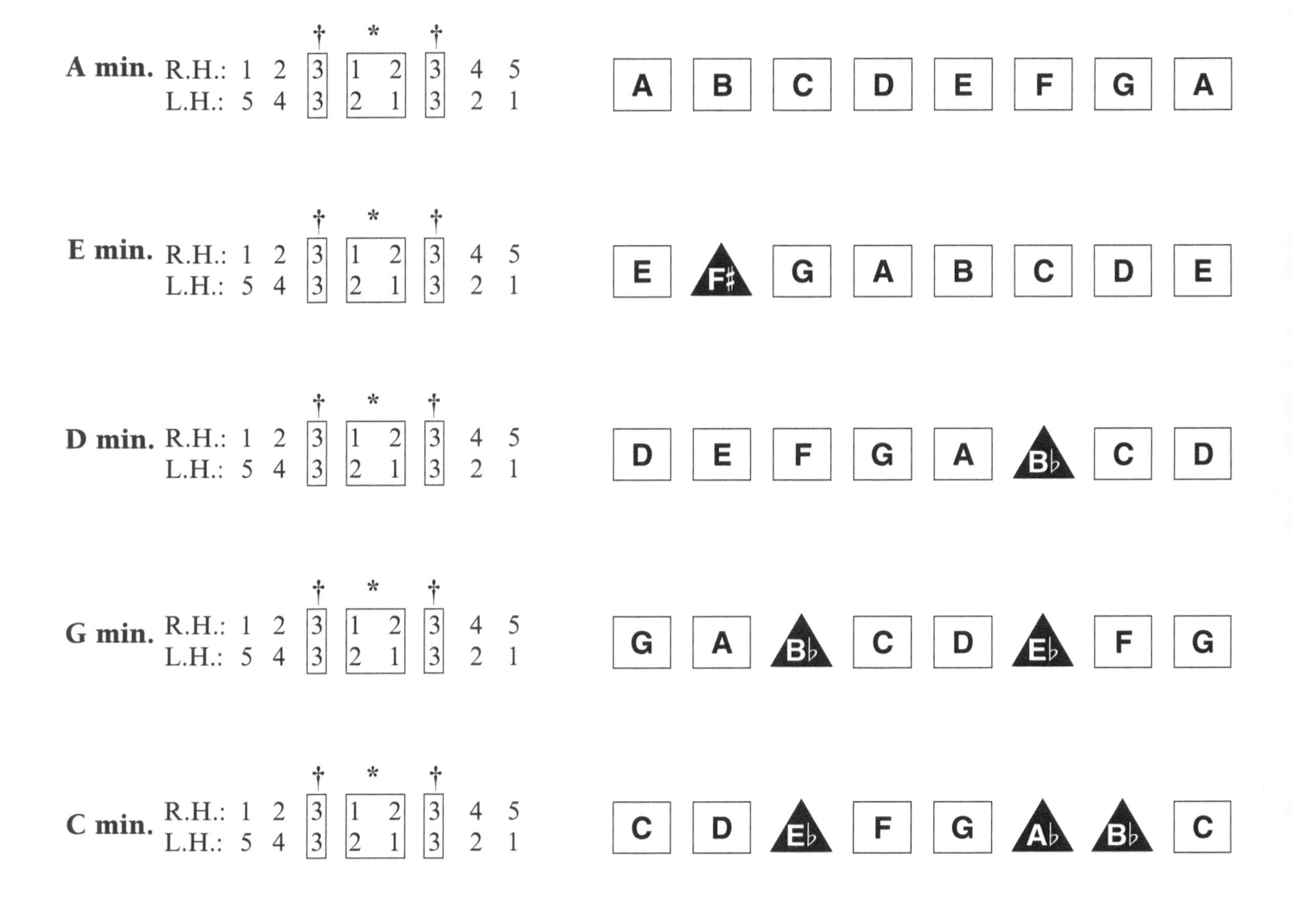

A min. R.H.: 1 2 3 1 2 3 4 5
L.H.: 5 4 3 2 1 3 2 1

A B C D E F G A

E min. R.H.: 1 2 3 1 2 3 4 5
L.H.: 5 4 3 2 1 3 2 1

E F♯ G A B C D E

D min. R.H.: 1 2 3 1 2 3 4 5
L.H.: 5 4 3 2 1 3 2 1

D E F G A B♭ C D

G min. R.H.: 1 2 3 1 2 3 4 5
L.H.: 5 4 3 2 1 3 2 1

G A B♭ C D E♭ F G

C min. R.H.: 1 2 3 1 2 3 4 5
L.H.: 5 4 3 2 1 3 2 1

C D E♭ F G A♭ B♭ C

- Notice that all the minor scales above have exactly the same fingering as the major scales with the same starting (tonic) notes. *Major and minor scales with the same starting notes are called parallel scales.*

FJH217

Group No. 2—F minor and B minor

- F minor has a different fingering in the **right hand** than the Group No. 1 scales.
- B minor has a different fingering in the **left hand** than the Group No. 1 scales.
- Notice that **thumbs of both hands** are played together in the middle of the scale.†

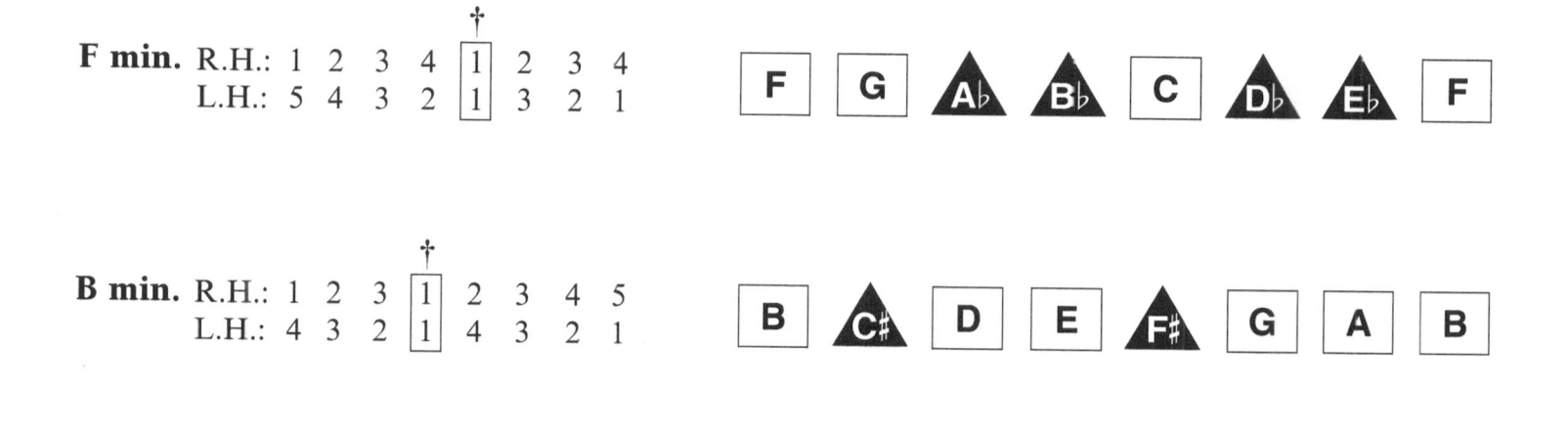

Group No. 3—F♯ minor and C♯ minor

- Always remember which key the *fourth finger* plays.
- Notice that the **third fingers** of both hands are always played at the same time.†
- Notice that the **first and second fingers** of both hands are played together in the middle of the scale, but the second finger in one hand plays at the same time as the first finger in the other hand.*

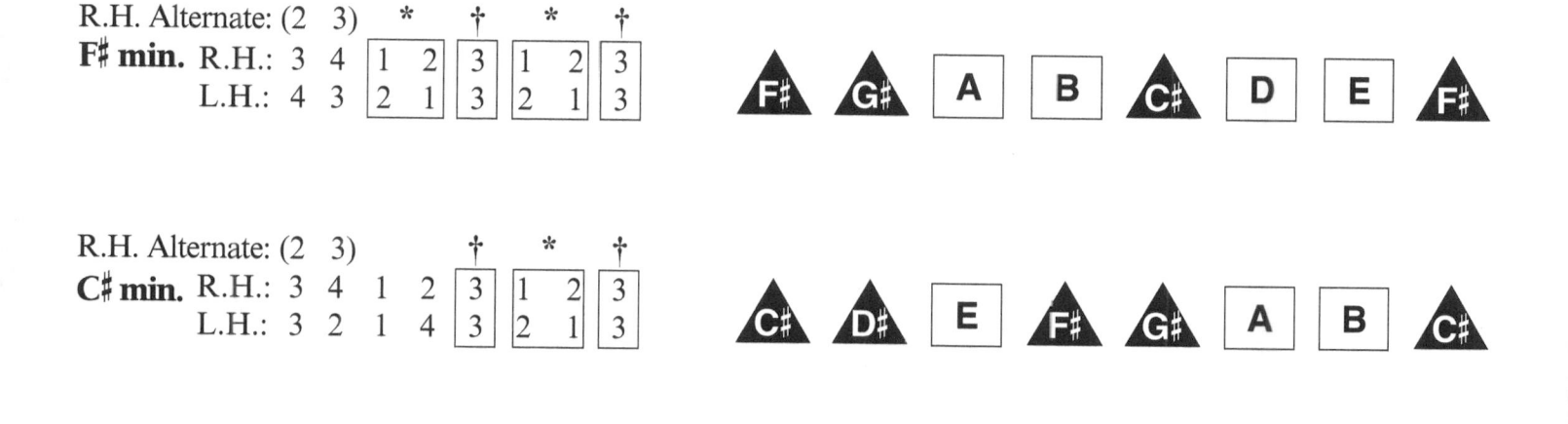

Group No. 4—B♭ minor, E♭ minor, and A♭ minor

- The *fourth finger in the right hand* always plays B♭. ⋄
- The *thumbs of both hands* always play together. †

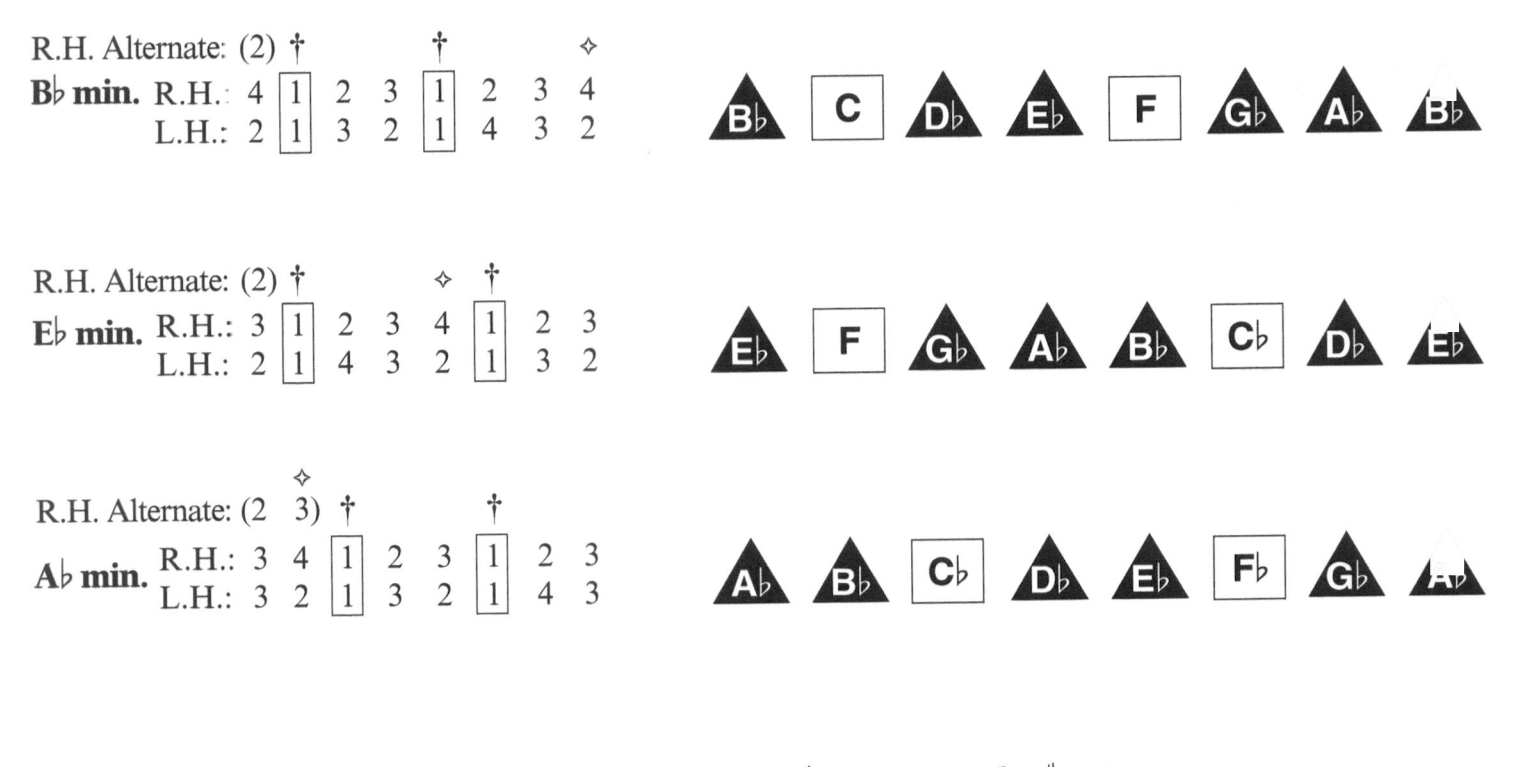

Group No. 5—G♯ minor, D♯ minor, and A♯ minor

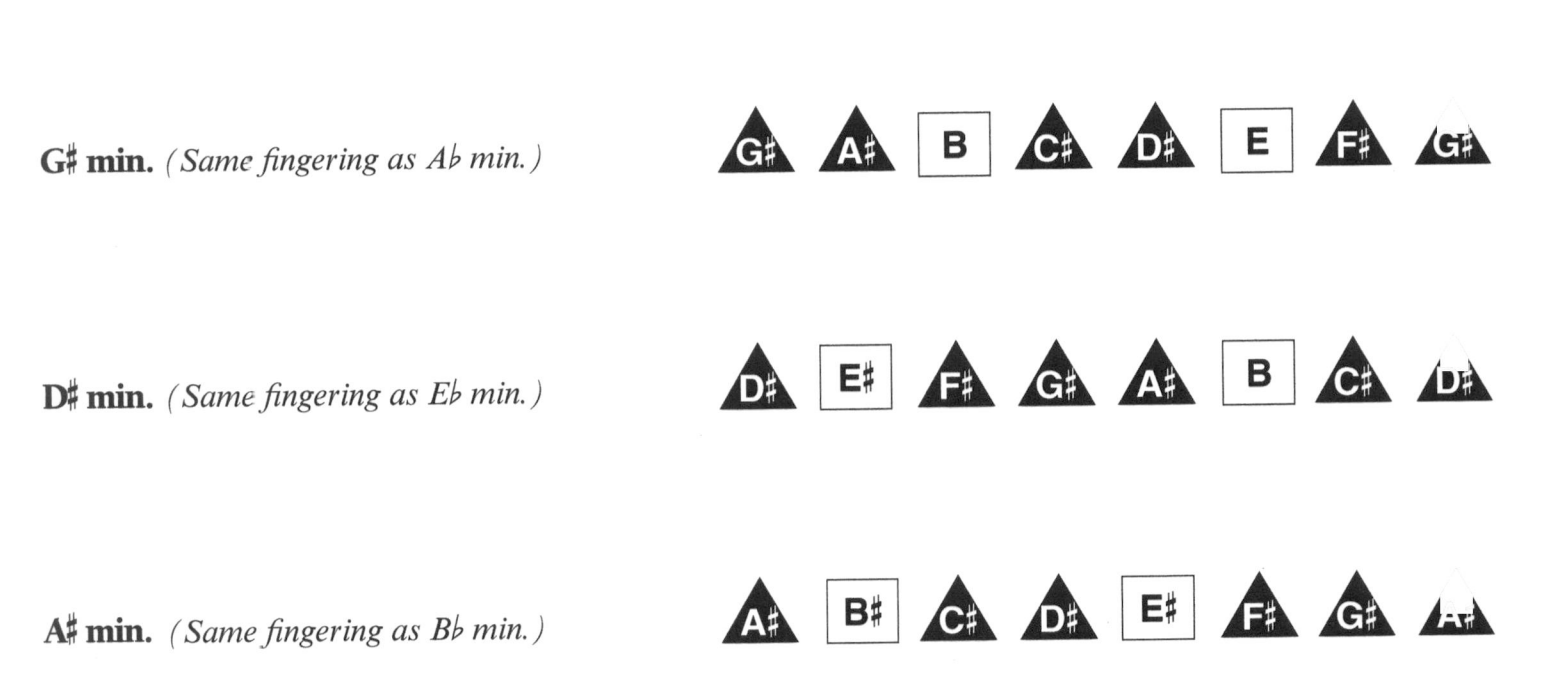

Scales that can have two different names are called *enharmonic scales*. For example, the C♯ scale uses the same sounding pitches as the D♭ scale, but with different note spellings.

FJH2175

Practice Suggestions for Playing Natural Minor Scales

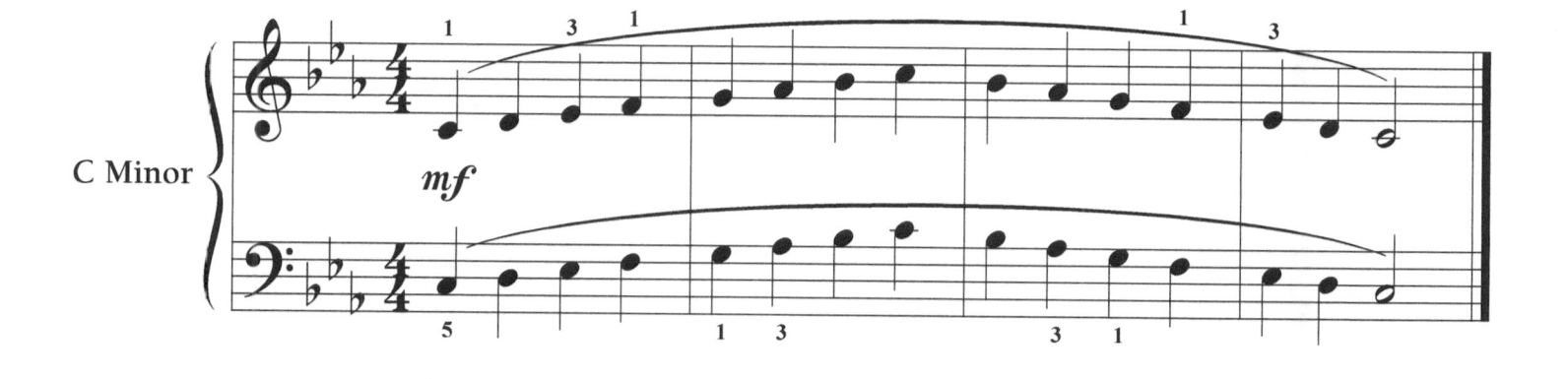

C Minor

1. Practice hands separately, listening for a beautiful sound.

2. Once secure with the fingering, practice hands together. Think about the patterns of white and black keys and which fingers play at the same time (refer to pages 22-24.)

3. For every minor scale, think about which key your *fourth finger* plays. It will always be the same key within each scale. (For example, in a D natural minor scale, the R.H. fourth finger ONLY plays C, while the L.H. fourth finger ONLY plays E.)

4. Practice the scales *legato* and evenly.

5. Practice at many different dynamic levels, such as *pp, p, mp, f*.

6. Practice one hand *f*, the other hand, *p*. Then switch hands.

7. *Crescendo* as you ascend to the highest note of the scale, and then *decrescendo* as you descend.

8. Always practice using the metronome:

   M.M. ♩ = _____   M.M. ♩ = _____   M.M. ♪ = _____ (teacher's choice)
                                         (faster)

Build up your speed weekly and you will play with a wonderful technique!

Technique Tips:

Practicing scales is always exciting because the ways you can practice are seemingly endless! You can play your scales:

1. By groups (pp. 22-24)

2. Through the Circle of Fifths: C G D A E B F♯(G♭) D♭ A♭ E♭ B♭ F (p. 43)

3. Chromatically (by half steps): C C♯ D D♯ E F F♯ G G♯ A A♯ B C

Technique Tip #1

Sit far enough away from the piano so that your elbows and arms move freely. Place your hands over the middle of the white keys—can you swing from left to right easily with your elbows hanging comfortably? Let your shoulders swing easily from the shoulder joint. Sit tall, with your shoulders low and wide. What you don't want to see are your elbows right next to your body or shoulders rounded and shrugged forward.

You can lean slightly forward from your hips into the keyboard with your upper torso. Your elbows will be toward the front of your body on either side. This will give you more power at the keyboard and help you play technically well.

Jennifer is the student pictured in this book. She studies with Dr. Marlais.

Technique Tip #2

Play with your wrists parallel to your forearm and with the floor. The tip of your elbow should be at the same height or slightly higher than the top of the white keys. Look in a mirror as you are playing or ask someone to look at you. If you are too low, place a few books on top of the piano bench, or buy extended legs for your bench.

Never play with low and locked wrists, or high and locked wrists!

Technique Tip #3

Use a flexible wrist and transfer the weight of your hand and forearm from one finger to the next as you play. The weight of your hand and arm should be directly centered over each finger so your arm supports each finger that plays. This is "weight transfer."

Technique Tip #4

Use arm weight when playing with your thumbs, being careful to land on the outside tip of your thumbnail so the sound isn't heavy but you play in a relaxed, tension-free way.

Let your thumb play alongside your other fingers, and don't push your thumb underneath your palm, because this causes tension. Be sure your wrist is flexible because your thumb needs to move quickly and loosely.

Technique Tip #5

Play with strong fingers—ones that do not dent in at the first knuckle joint. Form a strong bridge with the eight knuckles rounded on the top of your hands. Keep in mind to not collapse your knuckles or let your 4th and 5th fingers slope down. Stand almost completely tall on your fifth fingers.

Technique Tip #6

Roll your wrist in the direction of the notes. If the notes in the scales move up, roll to the right. If the notes in the scale move down, roll to the left. Lead with your elbow, letting your arm follow in the same direction.

Technique Tip #7

When playing the black keys, move your forearms and hands forward, toward the fallboard of the piano. This weight transfer technique will keep you from reaching or stretching for keys and help you to play quickly and easily.

Technique Tip #8

Always listen to yourself play evenly and with a beautiful tone. Always play with a steady rhythm. Using the metronome is a very good idea.

A Step-by-Step Approach to Playing a Minor Scale—(this takes focus!)

1. Place your fingers on the keys. Prepare your fingers over the black key(s) so you don't reach for them when it is time to play them.

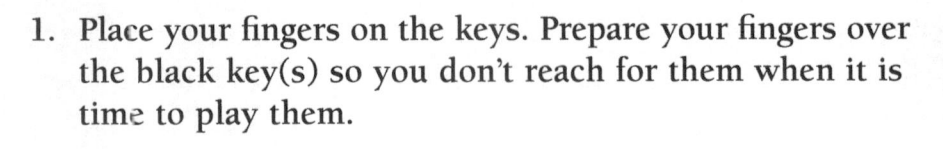

G minor Scale

2. Your thumb is loose and sits on the outside tip. Curve the thumb slightly towards your 2nd finger. Look for rounded fingers but not overly curved fingers.

   The arch of the hand is high and level with your forearm. Form a strong bridge with your four knuckles distinctly showing at the top of your hand. These four knuckles look like hills. Keep in mind to not collapse your knuckles when playing or let your 4th and 5th fingers slope down. Your fifth finger stands on its finger pad. Look down on your fifth finger and notice the first and second knuckle joints do not dent in.

3. Look for a backwards letter "C" between your thumb and second fingers.

4. Drop your thumb and wrist into the first key on the outside tip of the nail.

5. Roll your wrist, hand, and forearm in the direction of the ascending notes. The weight of your hand and forearm should be directly centered over each finger so your arm supports each finger that plays. This is "weight transfer." Play on your finger pads and not on your fingertips.

6. Your thumb follows the rest of the fingers as soon as it is lifted from the key. Make sure it is loose and not sticking out. As your 2nd and 3rd fingers play, raise your wrist slightly. When your 3rd finger plays, loosely place your 2nd finger next to finger 3. Notice that the top knuckle of your 2nd finger is straight in front of you. Be sure that your thumb hangs loosely behind fingers 2 and 3.

7. The hand, wrist, and forearm are aligned in a diagonal fashion. This proper alignment is essential for healthy, body-friendly scale technique. The thumb continues to slide to the right and prepares the fourth note of the scale. The 3rd finger acts as a pivot—just like a basketball player pivots on a foot to turn.

8. Drop your thumb on the outside tip on the fourth note of the scale, being careful not to make an accent. Immediately when the thumb is played, shift your hand to the right and prepare fingers 2, 3, 4, and 5 over the next four keys. (Your thumb is the pivot now.)

9. Roll your wrist in the direction of the last four notes. Keep your forearm moving in the direction of the notes. If there is a black key(s) in the scale, slightly raise your forearm to the key so you don't reach or stretch.

10. Stand tall on your fifth finger at the top of the scale. Play with a firm tip. Notice all five fingers relaxed and loosely next to each other. There are no "fly-away" fingers. Rest all five fingers lightly on the top of the keys. Your four knuckles are visible, like four little hills.

To play a **descending scale** with the **right hand**:

1. Roll your wrist in the direction of the descending notes. This is an "over the keys" motion across the five keys and not an "under the keys" motion, i.e., it is important in this motion to roll the wrist slightly up and around in the direction of the descending notes, and not keep the wrist low or too tight. Use weight transfer again to support each finger that plays with your arm.

2. Drop your thumb on the outside tip, being careful not to make an accent. Listen for a smooth line and even tone.

3. Immediately when the thumb is played, crossover with fingers 3 and 2, preparing them over the next two keys. Fingers 3 and 2 crossover as one playing unit.

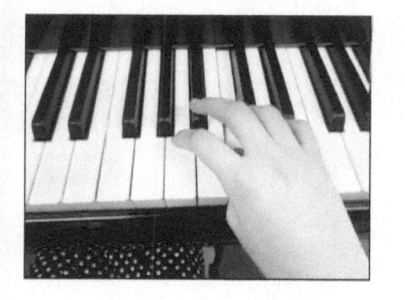

4. Watch fingers 3 and 2 roll to the left over your thumb. In crossing over, the thumb rolls so the fingers cross freely over the thumb. Roll on the outside tip of the thumb.

5. When playing your 3rd finger, quickly slide the thumb to the left (don't keep it under your palm) and prepare the last two keys of the scale.

6. Align your hand directly behind finger number 2.

7. Drop on the last note of the scale and then lift until the wrist is parallel to your forearm.

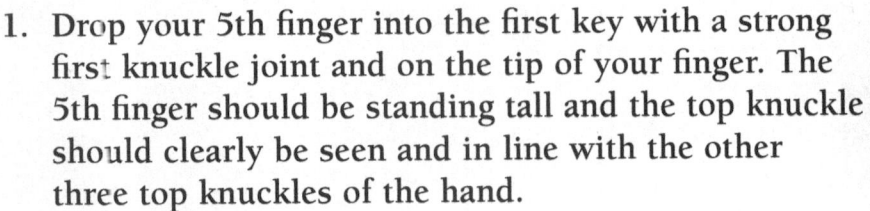

1. Drop your 5th finger into the first key with a strong first knuckle joint and on the tip of your finger. The 5th finger should be standing tall and the top knuckle should clearly be seen and in line with the other three top knuckles of the hand.

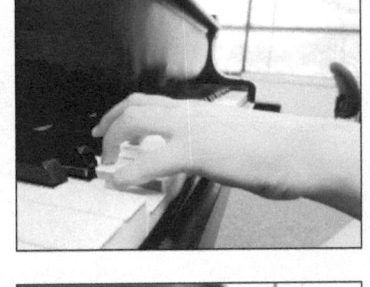

2. Roll your wrist in the direction of the ascending notes. This is an "over the keys" motion across the five keys and not an "under the keys" motion. The weight of your hand and forearm should be directly centered over each finger so your arm supports each finger that plays. This is "weight transfer." As your 4th 3rd fingers play, raise your wrist slightly.

3. Your hand, wrist, and forearm continue to roll to the right. Drop your thumb on the outside tip, being careful not to make an accent. Immediately when the thumb is played, crossover with fingers 3 and 2, preparing them over the next two keys. Fingers 3 and 2 crossover as one playing unit and they roll over the thumb. The thumb rolls from left to right.

4. Watch fingers 3 and 2 roll to the right over your thumb. Quickly slide the thumb to the right when playing your 3rd finger and prepare the last two keys of the scale.

5. Stand tall on your thumb at the top of the scale. Notice all five fingers relaxed and loosely next to each other. There are no "fly-away" fingers. Rest all five fingers lightly on the top of the keys. Look for the letter "C" between your thumb and second finger.

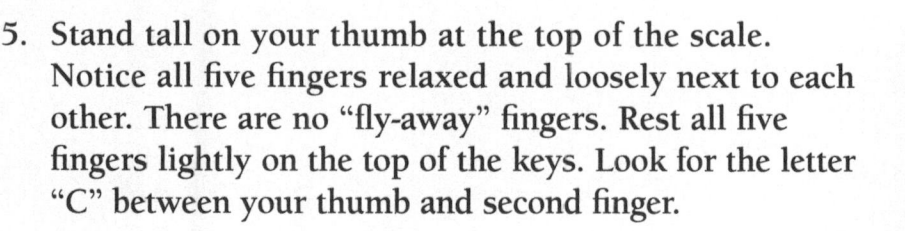

To play a **descending G natural minor scale** with the **left hand**:

1. Roll your wrist in the direction of the descending notes. This is an "over the keys" motion across the first three keys and not an "under the keys" motion. Use weight transfer again to support each finger that plays with your forearm.

2. Loosely place your 1st and 2nd fingers next to finger 3 as you roll your wrist over and to the left.

3. Stand tall on your 3rd finger in the middle of the scale. Notice all five fingers relaxed and loosely next to each other. There are no "fly-away" fingers. Rest your 5th, 4th, and 2nd fingers lightly on the top of the keys. Let your thumb rest on the same note on which your 2nd finger rests.

4. Roll your wrist in the direction of the descending notes. The weight of your hand and forearm should be directly centered over each finger so your arm supports each finger that plays. This is "weight transfer." Your thumb should start to move alongside the other fingers as soon as it is lifted from the key.

   This proper alignment is essential for healthy, body-friendly scale technique. (Be sure that your thumb hangs loosely behind fingers 2 and 3.)

5. The thumb continues to slide and prepares the fourth note of the scale.

6. Drop your thumb on the outside tip, being careful not make an accent.

7. Immediately when the thumb is played, shift your weight of your forearm and prepare fingers 2, 3, 4, and 5 over the next four keys.

8. Roll your wrist in the direction of the last four notes. This is an "over the keys" motion across the last five keys and not an "under the keys" motion.

9. Drop on the last note of the scale and then lift until the wrist is parallel to your forearm.

   Your practice must be regular in order to develop this physical skill. Once your brain and body remember this skill, you will become more fluent and will play spontaneously and comfortably. This is when piano playing becomes more fun!

More Practice Suggestions for Playing Minor Scales

- Transpose to all keys.

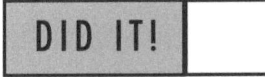

1. Accent the Strong Beats.

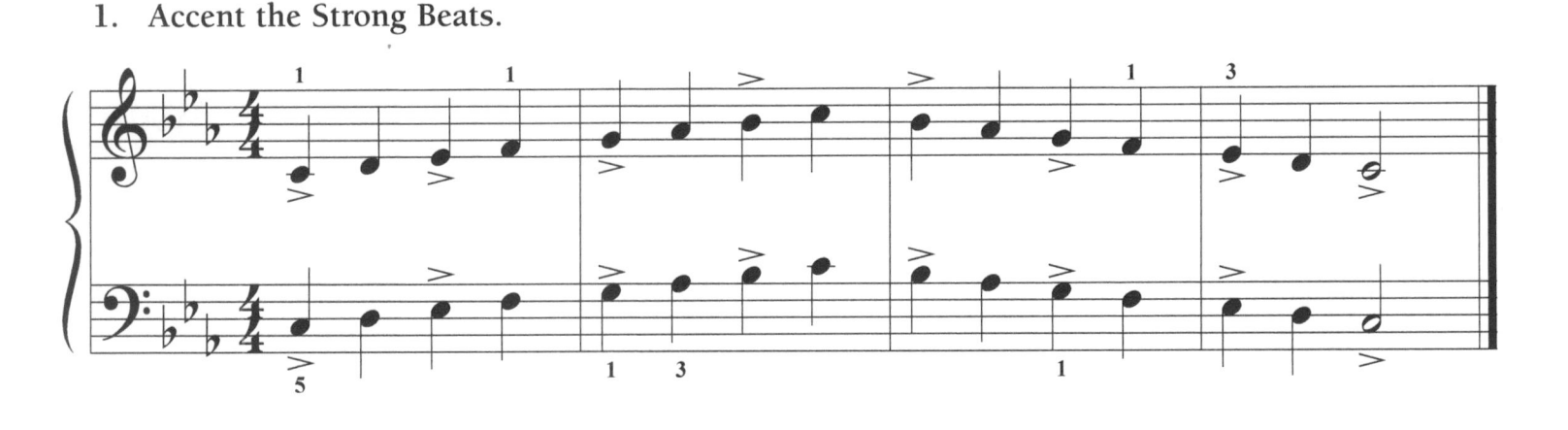

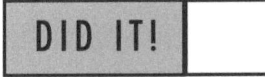

2. Accent the Weak Beats.

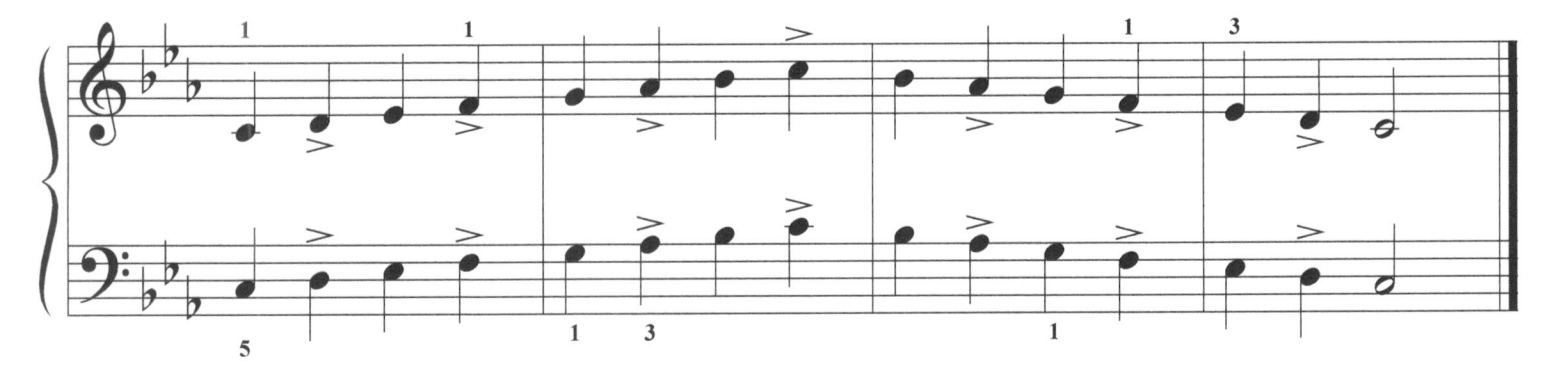

3. Move Hands in Contrary Motion.

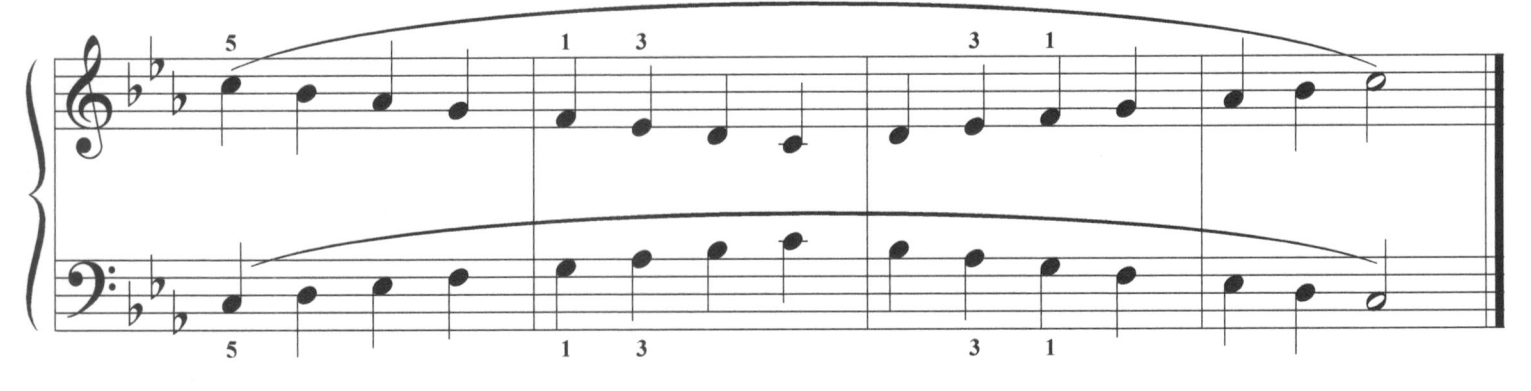

FJH2175

4. **Play with Mixed Quarter- and Eighth-Note Rhythms.**

5. **Slur Pairs of Notes Together.**

6. **Play with *legato* in the R.H. and *staccato* in the L.H.**
   (Play at a slower speed.)

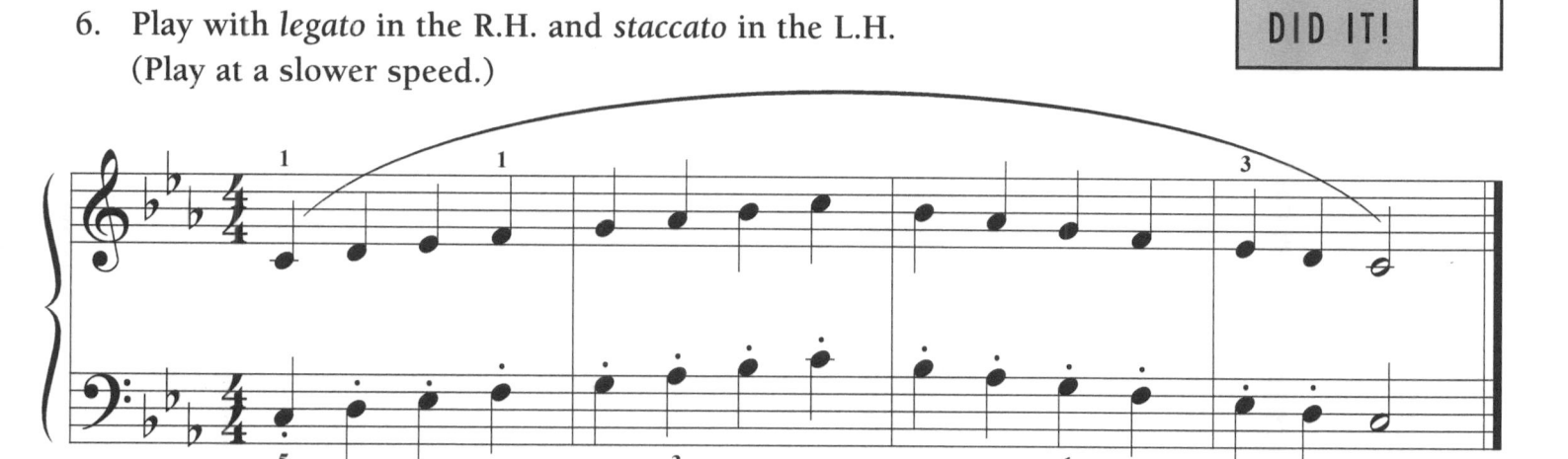

7. Play with *staccato* in the R.H. and *legato* in the L.H.
   (Play at a slower speed.)

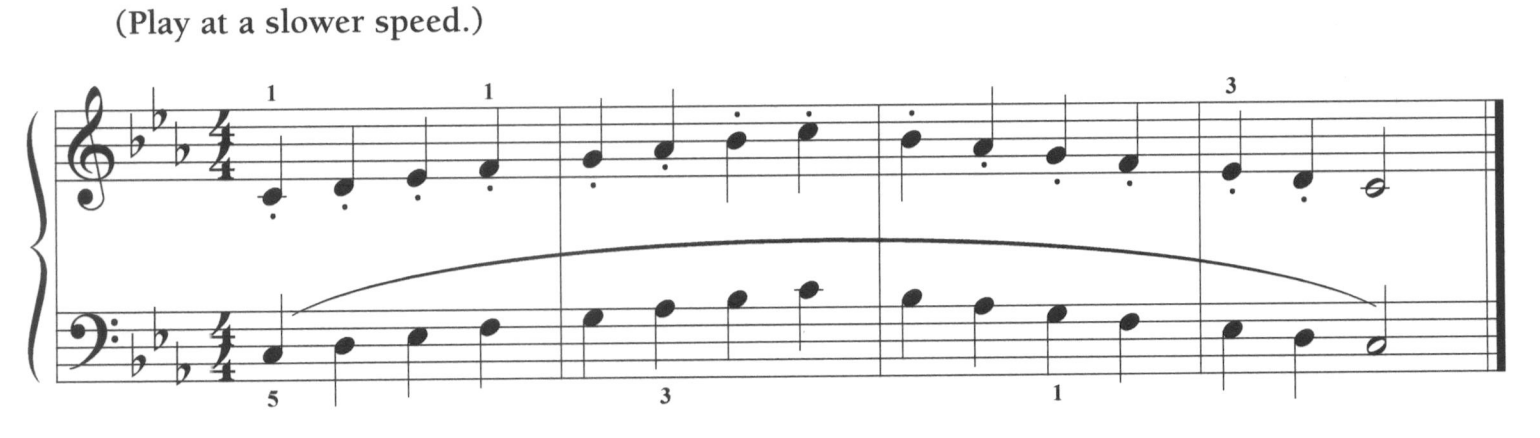

8. Play Using Dotted Quarter-Note Rhythm.

9. Play Descending First, then Ascending.

34

Fingering Charts for Minor Arpeggios

To remember them more easily, minor key arpeggios can be placed in the following groups:

☐ = white keys   ▲ = black keys

	PATTERN	FINGERING	HELPFUL HINTS
GROUP No. 1 C, F and G minor	☐ ▲ ☐	R.H. 1-2-3-5 L.H. 5-4-2-1	The Same Fingering as C Major

	PATTERN	FINGERING	HELPFUL HINTS
GROUP No. 2 A, D and E minor B minor E♭ minor	☐ ☐ ☐ ☐ ☐ ▲ ▲ ▲ ▲	R.H. 1-2-3-5 L.H. 5-4-2-1	The Same Fingering as C Major

	PATTERN	FINGERING	HELPFUL HINTS
GROUP No. 3 C♯, F♯ and A♭ minor	▲ ☐ ▲	R.H. 2-1-2-4 L.H. 2-1-4-2	Start with the 2nd fingers. Both thumbs play together.

	PATTERN	FINGERING	HELPFUL HINTS
GROUP No. 4 B♭ minor	▲ ▲ ☐	R.H. 2-3-1-2 L.H. 3-2-1-3	The 2nd and 3rd fingers play opposite each other. Both thumbs play together.

More Practice Suggestions for Playing Minor Arpeggios

(Try a different one every day and transpose to different keys.)

1. Play in Half and Quarter Notes.

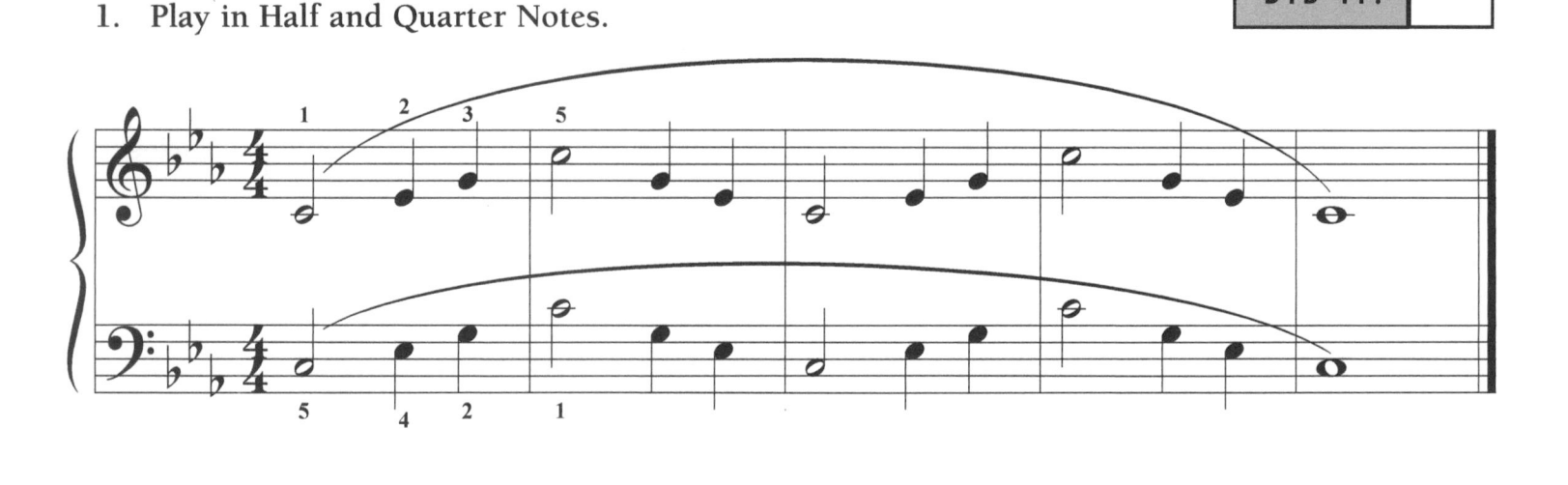

2. Play in Eighth Notes.

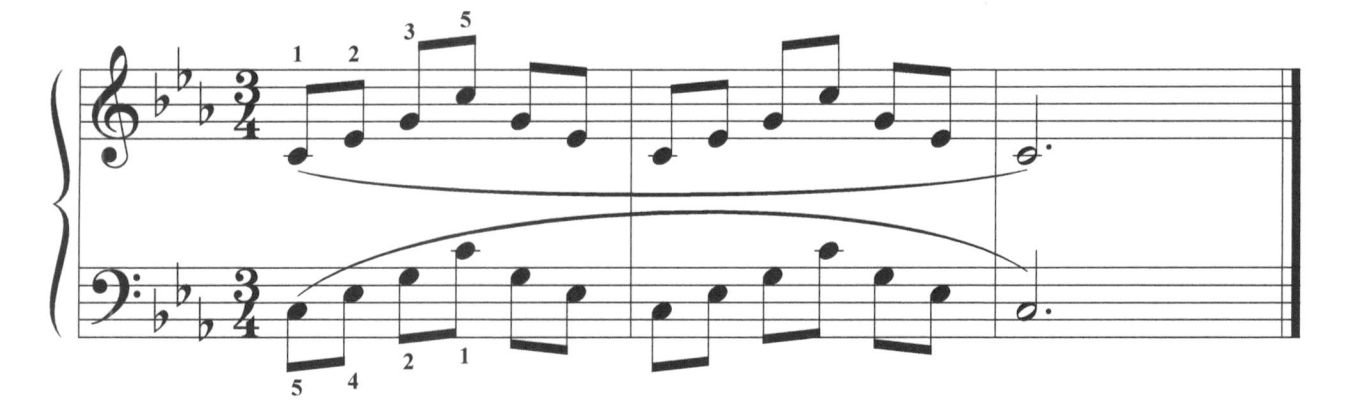

All arpeggios are not fingered alike—please refer to p. 35.

FJH2175

3. Play Each Note Twice (slurring one pitch to the next).

4. Play in Contrary Motion.

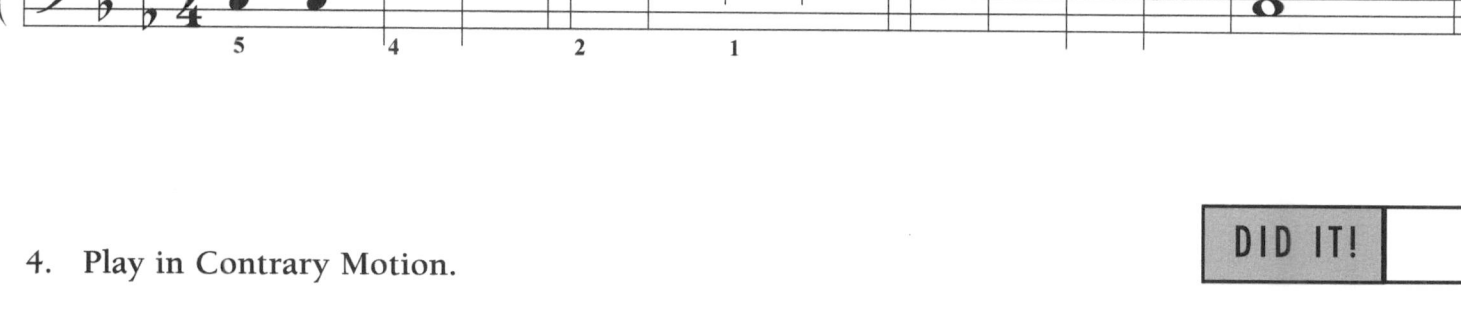

5. Exercises in Preparation for Playing a Two-Octave Arpeggio.
   (Play each hand separately at first, then hands together.)

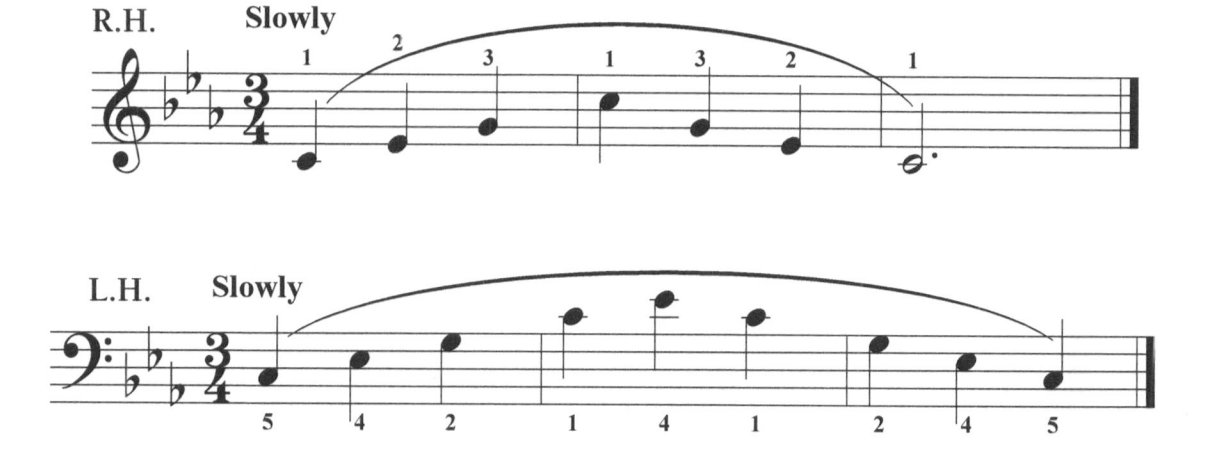

It's Time to Begin The Octave Scale, Cadence, and Arpeggio Countdown!

- Complete all five of the following games to confirm your skill!
  (Your teacher might time each game with a clock!)

- Move from one exercise to another—accuracy is your goal!

- Play evenly with a big, beautiful sound.

Countdown No. 1:

1. Play an A minor scale.

2. Play an A minor cadence.

3. Play an A minor arpeggio.

4. Play a D minor scale.

5. Play a D minor cadence

6. Play a D minor arpeggio.

7. Play an E minor scale.

8. Play an E minor cadence.

Teacher's Comments:

_____

_____

_____

_____

_____

_____

FJH2175

It's Time to Begin The Octave Scale, Cadence, and Arpeggio Countdown!

- Complete the next four games to confirm your skill!
  (Your teacher might time each game with a clock!)

- Move from one exercise to another—accuracy is your goal!

- Play evenly with a big, beautiful tone (sound.)

Countdown No. 2:

1. Play a C minor scale.

2. Play a C minor cadence.

3. Play a C minor arpeggio.

4. Play an F minor arpeggio.

5. Play an F minor cadence.

6. Play an F minor arpeggio.

7. Play a G minor scale.

8. Play a G minor cadence.

Teacher's Comments:

_____

_____

_____

_____

_____

_____

It's Time to Begin The Octave Scale, Cadence, and Arpeggio Countdown!

- Complete the next three games to confirm your skill!
  (Your teacher might time each game with a clock!)

- Move from one exercise to another—accuracy is your goal!

- Play evenly with a big, beautiful tone (sound.)

Countdown No. 3:

1. Play the C Major scale, and then the A minor scale.

2. Play the F Major scale, and then the D minor scale.

3. Play the G Major scale, and then the E minor scale.

4. Play the D Major scale, and then the B minor scale.

5. Play the cadence of your teacher's choice.

6. Play one arpeggio of your teacher's choice.

** Extra Credit: Play the scale, cadence, and arpeggio of your teacher's choice.

Teacher's Comments:

_____

_____

_____

_____

_____

_____

FJH2175

It's Time to Begin The Octave Scale, Cadence, and Arpeggio Countdown!

- Complete the next two games to confirm your skill!
  (Your teacher might time each game with a clock!)

- Show your teacher how excellent your technique is!

- Move from one exercise to another—accuracy is your goal!

- Play evenly with a big, beautiful tone (sound.)

Countdown No. 4:

1. Play the C minor, F minor, and G minor arpeggios.

2. Play the A minor, D minor, and E minor arpeggios.

3. Play the B♭ Major scale, and then the G minor scale.

4. Play the E♭ Major scale, and then the C minor scale.

5. Play the A♭ minor cadence.

6. Play the C♯ minor cadence.

7. Play one scale of your teacher's choice.

8. Play one arpeggio of your teacher's choice.

Teacher's Comments:

_____

_____

_____

_____

_____

_____

It's Time to Begin The Octave Scale, Cadence, and Arpeggio Countdown!

- Complete the last game to confirm your skill!

- Move from one exercise to another—accuracy is your goal!

- Play evenly with a big, beautiful tone (sound.)

Countdown No. 5:

1. Play the B♭ minor scale.

2. Play the B♭ minor cadence.

3. Play the E♭ Major scale.

4. Play the E♭ minor cadence.

5. Play the A♭ minor scale.

6. Play the A♭ minor cadence.

7. Play the C♯ minor scale.

8. Play the C♯ minor cadence.

** Extra Credit: Play the scale, cadence, and arpeggio of your teacher's choice.

Teacher's Comments:

_____

_____

_____

_____

_____

_____

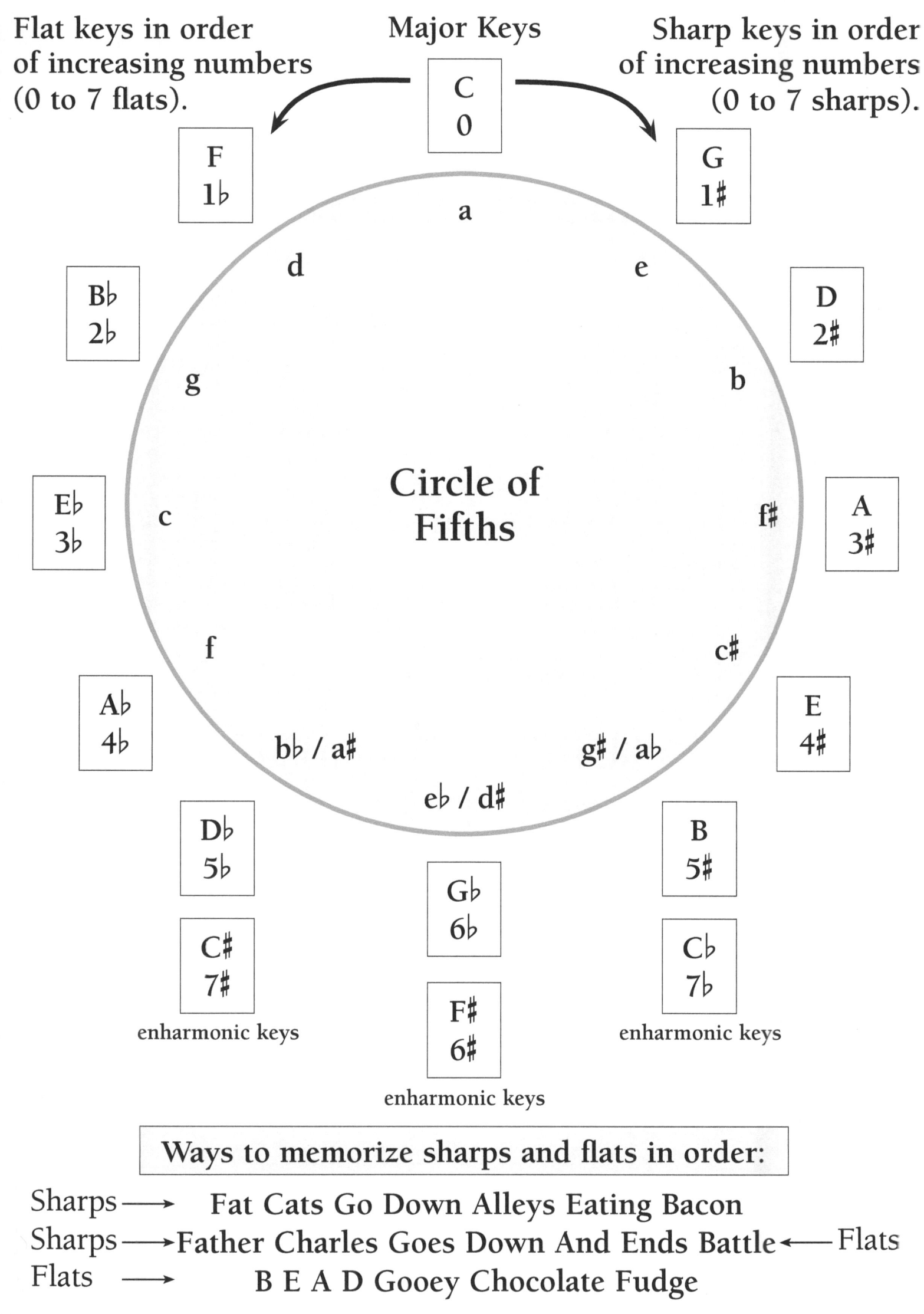

Flat keys in order of increasing numbers (0 to 7 flats).

Major Keys

Sharp keys in order of increasing numbers (0 to 7 sharps).

C 0

F 1♭

G 1#

B♭ 2♭

D 2#

E♭ 3♭

A 3#

A♭ 4♭

E 4#

D♭ 5♭

B 5#

C# 7#

C♭ 7♭

enharmonic keys

enharmonic keys

G♭ 6♭

F# 6#

enharmonic keys

Circle of Fifths

a

d

e

g

b

c

f#

f

c#

b♭ / a#

g# / a♭

e♭ / d#

Ways to memorize sharps and flats in order:

Sharps ⟶ Fat Cats Go Down Alleys Eating Bacon

Sharps ⟶ Father Charles Goes Down And Ends Battle ⟵ Flats

Flats ⟶ B E A D Gooey Chocolate Fudge

Certificate of Achievement

_____

has successfully completed

Play Your Scales and Chords Every Day®

BOOK 3

of The FJH Pianist's Curriculum®

You are now ready for **Book 4**

_____
Date

_____
Teacher's Signature

FJH2175